WILD CHICAGO

WILD
CHICAGO

Animals,
reptiles,
insects,
and plants
to watch
out for at
home, at the
park, and in
the woods

F. LYNNE BACHLEDA

CLERISY PRESS

WILD
CHICAGO

For further information, contact the publisher at:
Clerisy Press
306 Greenup Street
Covington, KY 41011
clerisypress.com
a division of Keen Communications

CATALOGING-IN-PUBLICATION DATA IS AVAILABLE FROM
THE LIBRARY OF CONGRESS
ISBN-13: 978-1-57860-529-3
eISBN: 978-1-57860-530-9

Distributed by Publishers Group West
Printed in the United States of America
First edition, first printing
Cover design by Scott McGrew
Text design by Stephen Sullivan

Cover photo credits:
(*top row*) massasauga snake—Wikimedia Commons, Tim Vickers;
northern black widow spider— Wikimedia Commons, James Gathany;
Canada geese— Wikimedia Commons, Pep1863.
(*bottom row*) wheel bug—Wikimedia Commons, jeffreyw;
white-tailed deer—Wikimedia Commons, Scott Bauer;
paper wasp—Wikimedia Commons, Bruce J. Marlin

Dedicated to the well-being of all.
And to my friends, who are my family.

contents

WATER SNAKE

POISON IVY

GREAT HORNED OWL

HONEYBEE

WHITE-TAILED BUCK

RED-TAILED HAWK

intro

Yes, it is a wild jungle out there. But mostly it's a fascinating, fun, beautiful, mysterious, and safe wild world. I hope that this book helps you appreciate all those dimensions of nature in the Chicago area. The real jungle may, in fact, be in your mind if you harbor irrational fears about what can harm you. I promise this book will help you separate myth from fact and replace fear with respect.

I want to encourage lots of happy, confident engagement with the natural world. Having this knowledge handy—in my head and also as a tangible ready reference—gives me a sense of assurance. I can also honestly say I think every home ought to have a copy because what's in this book can make your life easier and maybe even save it, too. But take heart, gentle readers. Many of the names in the stories in this book have been changed to protect the guilty. Most of this stuff happened to me. See? It really is hard to die out there. So read, absorb, relax, and enjoy. It truly is a marvelous and miraculous planet.

F. LYNNE BACHLEDA

mammals

We often like to forget the fact that we are mammals—warm-blooded creatures with body hair and females with mammary glands that secrete milk to nourish young. You might think that other mammals pose the greatest danger to you, and in one sense you would be dead right about that: we humans are by far the most dangerous mammals on earth. According to the F.B.I. an estimated 14,748 persons were murdered and manslaughtered nationwide in 2010. In comparison there were roughly 50 fatalities from exposure to animals including bats, cats, dogs, foxes, raccoons, rodents, lagomorphs (rabbits and hares), skunks, and other mammals.

That said, it is a very foolish person indeed who engages any wild animal. Don't make friendly overtures toward any wild species, plus dogs you don't know. Even field mice will bite, and they can carry disease and cause infection. So if you are tempted to rescue one from the jaws of your house cat, grab a dishtowel first to shield your hands. The panicked mouse will draw blood if it can—a perfect example of how an apparently innocent encounter with a wild animal—whose instincts drive an agenda quite different from yours—can turn nasty quickly.

Basically, Chicago-area mammals can affect you in a limited but powerful number of ways: bites, sprays, disease, and auto accidents.

biting mammals

When threatened or angered, we are all likely to use any means necessary to communicate our needs and passions. Most people can identify with the statement, "I just snapped." Other mammals, unable simply to slam a fist on the table in vexation, can snap, too.

Again, we want to stress the extreme unlikelihood of your encounter with the teeth of a wild animal unless you do something foolish—and our intent is to minimize that possibility. It is impossible, though, and not even desirable to take the risk out of dangerous or deadly encounters with animals. Such encounters are inescapable in nature. Animal expert Stephen Herrero argues the point about bears, but it applies to all wild animals: "You've got to have some tolerance to risk. You reduce it [risk] to zero, you've reduced the bears to zero, too."

CATS AND DOGS

The danger of a "close encounter of the fang kind" is greatest at home. Our companion animals, domestic dogs and cats, are many times more likely to bite humans than are their wild country cousins. Good Samaritans who are trying to help an injured dog or cat, even if it is their own pet, should be especially cautious. If it can be accomplished safely, injured dogs should be muzzled; otherwise it might be better to wait for animal control assistance.

"WILD THANG, I THINK YOU MOVE ME"

In nature, it's always good to expect the unexpected. Just ask former President Jimmy Carter. You may recall that he was attacked by a garden-variety rabbit while vacationing in Plains, Georgia. While fishing from a canoe in a pond, he spotted a rabbit with a real attitude swimming furiously toward him. Though the rabbit's problem was never identified precisely, Carter later speculated that the highly agitated lagomorph was fleeing a predator. Whatever the case, the rabbit was clearly troubled. "It was hissing menacingly, its teeth flashing and nostrils flared and making straight for the President," a press account said. Fortunately for all, Carter deflected the frenzied beast with his canoe paddle before the Secret Service was forced to plug the bunny to save the prez. The moral of the story is: It's a jungle out there. "En garde!"

THE INFLUENCE OF THE MOON ON ANIMAL BITES

In December 2000 *The British Medical Journal* reported the results of a study indicating a greater tendency for animals to bite people during a full moon. The study lumped all types of animal bites together, but the incidence-rate ratio of the bites for all other periods of the lunar cycle was significantly lower.

Biting the Hand That Pets You

The joys of sharing life with a pet can enrich your days beyond measure. Research amply documents that pets relieve anxiety in times of stress, as well as teach important lessons about life and responsibility. At any stage of our lives, animals enlighten us with vital, important, and positive messages, but they can have a special influence on a child's development. A pet's unconditional affection provides emotional continuity and perhaps even a lifeline for a child.

On the cautionary side, however, each year 800,000 Americans seek medical attention for dog bites; half of these are children. Of those injured, 386,000 require treatment in an emergency department and about 16 die. The rate of dog bite-related injuries is highest for children ages 5 to 9 years, and the rate decreases as children age. Almost two-thirds of injuries among children ages 4 years and younger are to the head or neck region. Injury rates in children are significantly higher for boys than for girls.

Cat bites run a distant second after dog bites. Cat bites, however, are much more likely to develop serious infection because of the types of bacteria they carry in their mouths. With all this biting going on, it seems practical and prudent to prevent the situations that tend to provoke our furry buddies.

Most bite victims are children, and they are likely to be bitten on the face. Because their natural exuberance may easily startle, overexcite, or threaten a pet, children should be instructed from a very early age on how to handle themselves around dogs and cats. Biting is a natural response for dogs and cats, so the responsibility falls to us—children and adults—to learn how to safely be around them.

All that said, let's put this in perspective. Dog attack fatalities remain extremely rare. Children are at much greater risk of drowning in a backyard pool or being murdered by a close relative or caregiver than they are of being killed by what will always be "man's best friend." More people are killed each year in the U.S. by either bees or lightning than by dogs, and this perspective should not be lost in a swell of anti-dog hysteria. One vet reports: "It's much more common for me to have to

{ mammals }

muzzle a cocker spaniel, dachshund, Jack Russell terrier, or Chihuahua for a routine exam than a pit bull or a rott[weiler]."

Guidelines for Preventing Cat and Dog Bites

Some of the directions below may seem overly cautious to dedicated animal lovers who generally make friends easily with dogs and cats. We have given you these more careful, extensive instructions, however, because we want to give you every tool possible for those encounters that turn menacing.

☞ Teach your children to apply the golden rule to animals. Respect for another creature is a valuable lesson animals have to offer, so make sure children know that a family pet is not simply another fuzzy toy but a creature that has needs and wants very similar to their own. Therefore, teach children that if an animal doesn't come to them, leave it alone. Animals that are handled gently are much more likely to respond in kind.

☞ Do not approach strange dogs or cats. If an animal is on a leash, ask the human if you may pet the dog or cat. Especially avoid a dog that is on a chain or tied up. Avoid contact with free-roaming animals.

☞ Always be gentle in your voice, touch, and movement around the animal.

☞ Do not approach dogs or cats quickly. If you startle them, they may run or attack.

☞ Don't pull on a cat's or dog's tail, ears, or neck, or physically harass the animal in any way.

☞ Teach children not to tease dogs or cats with sticks, food, or any other objects. Older children can be taught the fine line between teasing and playing with an animal and can learn the warning signs when playing turns into something more dangerous. Teasing even during play will unintentionally frustrate the dog or cat and may lead to biting.

☞ Growling is a dog's warning to stop whatever you are doing, but some dogs will bite without warning. Also cease and desist if a cat begins growling, snarling, hissing, or arching its back.

☞ Keep close watch on children when dogs or cats are in the same vicinity.

Preventing Cat Bites

☞ Many bites take place when a well-intentioned person tries to pick up or pet a stray cat. Any animal that is scared, perhaps starving, or feels cornered is likely to bite. When dealing with stray or feral kitties, be careful and wear gloves, or at minimum use a cloth or towel as a bite barrier.

☞ People are frequently bitten or scratched when they try to stop a fight between cats, or try to comfort a cat that is scared. A person in the wrong place at the wrong time can be a victim of a cat's redirected aggression. The cat is not actually mad at the person, but because the cat has already been aroused and is angry or fearful, it may attack any person or thing that comes near it.

☞ When a cat is cornered, forcing your attention on it will leave it no choice but to fight.

☞ Cats that are declawed may be more apt to become biters because one of their prime defense mechanisms for protection and escape has been eliminated. This point is controversial, but still worthy of consideration. If you feel you must declaw a cat, perhaps you should consider more carefully having a cat as a pet.

☞ Sometimes petting a cat on certain parts of its body will trigger an instinctive reaction to bite or scratch. One area, especially for unneutered males, is around the base of the tail. Another is the stomach. If your cat grabs or begins to bite your arm or hand while you are petting its stomach, do not immediately try to withdraw it as this will only excite the cat's instincts. Stop moving and wait for your cat to lose interest in this perceived threat.

Preventing Dog Bites

☞ Use reason in selecting a dog. Consider the traits of the breed and how well they will match the care, training, and supervision you can give it. Though a dog with a highly aggressive temperament may seem good for home security, it may not be compatible with small children who do not fully understand the dog's need for boundaries.

☞ When buying puppies from breeders, ask to see the parents of the dog to assess their temperaments.

☞ There is some consensus that properly weaned puppies should be separated from their dams and placed in their new homes at seven weeks of age for proper socialization. Prematurely separated puppies fail to be properly socialized by their dam and littermates. Yet some experts think delaying the process fosters "pack" mentality and behavior and interferes with the bonding to the new human family.

☞ When acquiring dogs of any age from the local animal shelter, try to determine how the animal interacts with other dogs, cats, and people of various ages and sizes. This can lessen the chance of an unsuitable match.

{ mammals }

7

- Properly socialize puppies, especially between 4 and 16 weeks of age, to prevent excessive fear and aggression toward strangers when they are adults. Young dogs need to learn how to be comfortable around other dogs, too, so take your puppy (on a leash at first) to places where he or she can learn to feel at ease around other dogs. *However, and this is important, contact with other dogs should be avoided until three weeks after the puppy completes a puppyhood vaccination series.* Distemper and parvovirus still kill a lot of unvaccinated dogs.

- Puppies naturally use their teeth when playing, but they must be discouraged from doing so on people even during play. Their chewing and "mouthing" should be corrected with a sharp "No" and the chewing redirected to an appropriate chew toy.

- Puppies and dogs should not be allowed to use their teeth when taking treats out of hands. To discourage this, offer the treat inside a closed fist. Only allow the dog to take the treat after it has gently nudged with its muzzle. Do not hold the treat above the dog's head, which would encourage it to jump up and grab the treat out of your hand.

- Teach children about any dangerous neighborhood animals and avoid routes where dogs are known to chase pedestrians or cyclists. Dogs are often prompted by motion, such as a person running or riding a bike.

- Dogs are also motivated by noise and are more likely to bite when the person yells or screams. If you do speak, do so in a low, firm voice.

- If an unleashed dog does approach your children, teach them not to panic but to stand with hands at their sides while being as quiet and as still as possible. Let the dog sniff; speak in a calm, low voice to the animal. The dog will probably move away, and the children can then also move away.

- If a dog starts to growl or show signs of aggression, back away. Do not turn and run, as you may trigger the dog's natural chase instinct. You may try to slowly back away. If this movement makes the dog more assertive or aggressive (moving toward you, growling, snarling), then you must stand still and very slowly move your hands and arms to protect your chest and neck. In this situation, only back away after the dog has left.

- Stare straight ahead if you encounter a dog running loose. Avoid eye contact with the dog because the dog may perceive this as a challenge. If a dog approaches you, do not stare at it. Instead, watch its movements out of the corner of your eye.

- If a dog approaches or runs toward you, stand still. You cannot outrun a dog. Running away will encourage the dog to chase you. Keep your movements and actions low-key and your voice firm but subdued.

- ☞ If you happen to be in a situation where a menacing stray dog approaches you aggressively, stand very still with your hands to your side and feet together. Or if you're on the ground, lie on your side, tucking your chin and knees to your chest and placing a fist over each ear. Be like a rock. If a dog knocks you down, do not move. Lie on your stomach and cover the back of your neck with your hands.
- ☞ Do not let children stick their fingers or hands through a fenced enclosure to pet a dog. Likewise, stay clear of dogs in parked cars or tied by a leash. The dog may feel especially defensive of its territory under these confining conditions.
- ☞ Never enter a fenced yard containing a dog if the owner is not there, and even then, not without the owner's permission.

Dog Fights

Trying to break up fighting dogs is a quick, sure, and easy way to get bitten. Instead of reaching into a swirling mass of flying fur and gnashing teeth, make an unexpected loud noise like honking a car horn. That may startle the animals into separating. Turning the hose on the dogs is another option, but some report limited effectiveness with this method. Otherwise, be patient, stay out of the way, and hope for the best.

Human Infants in a Home with Cats or Dogs

Sadly, many people automatically assume that having an animal in the home is incompatible with bringing home a new baby, so they "dispose" of their pet by giving it away or taking it to a shelter where odds are good it will be killed. This is simply not necessary. With a small amount of effort, your animal can adapt quite well to the presence of the baby in the house, perhaps even coming to the baby's aid in times of need. Stories of how dogs and cats like to "watch over" young children are quite common. You should never, however, leave an infant (or a young child) alone with an animal, especially a dog. You may think the risk of danger is low, but the stakes are far too high for gambling.

All that said, most animals adjust with ease to the new arrival. Throughout this book, we try to give you every possible tool for success, but please do not misread this amount of topic coverage as an indicator of the likelihood of trouble. The longstanding human-animal bond is mutually rewarding and beneficial, and the odds are excellent that your creatures will adapt just fine.

{ mammals }

Regarding Cats and Dogs

☞ To begin the transition of bringing a newborn into the house, send something home from the hospital as soon as possible that smells of the baby. Let the dog or cat sniff this so that when the baby comes it will not be quite so strange or interesting. You can augment this by letting the animal smell the other aromas associated with newborns such as lotions and powders.

☞ When you come home from the hospital, have someone else carry the baby into the house. Your pet will have missed you in your absence, and this way you can devote some critical first minutes with your dog or cat to reassure them that you still have a special place in your heart for them.

☞ Remember that along with your baby, your dog or cat needs you, too! Spare at least a few minutes every day for special attention to your pet.

☞ You can't keep your infant and your pet apart forever, so let them meet as soon and as often as possible. Give the animal plenty of treats during this introductory time so that it will associate being in the presence of the baby as a pleasant experience and nothing to worry about.

☞ Each new experience you have with the baby (crying, feeding, bathing, etc.) is also a new experience for your pet, so simply let your pet see what the commotion is about. If you exclude pets, you may initiate resentment toward the child.

☞ For your children's safety, you must teach them not to mistreat animals in any way, because even the slightest cruelty might provoke a trusted pet. An old woman wise in the ways of animals observed, "I bet they get headaches and have bad days, too."

Regarding Cats

☞ Pregnant women should avoid coming into contact with the cat's litter box because it is a source of toxoplasmosis, an infection caused by a protozoan that can cause mental retardation and other medical problems in the developing fetus. (Another source is handling or eating raw meat, which pregnant women are also advised to avoid.) Pregnant women should have their partners change the litter box. If a pregnant woman must do it herself, she should wear gloves and a mask, as the protozoan responsible for toxoplasmosis can be airborne. Scoop the litter boxes of indoor/outdoor cats daily to decrease or even eliminate the risk of "toxo"; the infective life-cycle stage requires at least a day after being shed by the cat to become infectious.

☞ It's a myth that cats will inadvertently suffocate a baby while sniffing for milk on the baby's lips, or that cats will attack an infant when it cries, thinking another cat is in the house. (It's much more likely that a cat will run from such a wailing.) After a period of adjustment, you may find your cat cuddled up with your child. This is a classic illustration of a cat seeking warm, lazy comfort (for which cats are notorious)—not the beginning of a coup on the crown prince (or princess). If this behavior is a concern, use netting over the crib to prevent the cat's entry.

Regarding Dogs

☞ You have months of foreknowledge that a child is coming, so use the time to prepare the dog by establishing proper behavior boundaries.

☞ If the dog sleeps with you, you may want to train it to stay off the bed for those times that the newborn will be with you there.

☞ If a dog jumps freely on the furniture when it pleases, it could inadvertently leap onto the baby one day.

☞ Train your dog to respond to basic commands properly. It will be extra difficult to carry a baby around and have a dog that completely ignores you when you need it to sit-stay or down-stay, for example.

☞ Dogs that jump up on people can easily and inadvertently injure a baby carried in someone's arms.

☞ You might need to leave a room with the baby, leaving the dog behind. Make sure your dog already accepts being left in one room while you are elsewhere in the house.

☞ On the first encounter after arriving home from the hospital, greet the dog without the baby in your arms (as above), and then perhaps put it outside while you get the baby settled. Then bring the dog back inside on leash and let it satisfy its curiosity in the new arrival. Because newborn babies are essentially boring, the dog will probably quickly lose interest. Someone could play a quick game with the dog or take it for a walk fairly quickly after the homecoming to lower the already high-energy level of the house on such an important day.

☞ Without the proper attention, it is possible, though not likely, that your pet will become jealous of your newborn. To reassure your old friend, spend some time on the floor with your baby on your lap. Without pressuring your dog, invite her or him to come to you for some affection. This will give the animal a chance to satisfy its curiosity about the baby and diminish its concern over being replaced. Don't, however, force closeness.

{ mammals }

11

☞ All dogs do not immediately comprehend an infant as a human. Most dogs will adapt with no problems, but if your dog has a reputation by breed or temperament toward aggression, or is especially prone to bringing down small prey, be especially watchful until you know how the new relationship is sorting itself out. Because you will never leave the infant alone with the dog, this should not prove to be a problem.

☞ You're at a critical stage of child-dog relations when babies start learning how to move around. Children are fascinated with the dogs, moving towards them and sometimes cornering a dog that has no means of escape. Babies grab things, including the dog, to pull themselves up, and they may fall on sleeping dogs or grab the dog's toys away. Be especially sensitive to your dog's needs at this time. You may have to keep the dog's toys off the floor while the child is "loose" to prevent possessiveness.

If You Are Bitten by a Cat or Dog

If a dog or cat bites you or your child, seek medical aid as soon as possible. Try to remember the circumstances of the attack, the description of the animal, and, if possible, obtain the owner's name and address. Later, when you speak to the owner, try to ascertain whether the animal has had a current rabies vaccination. All of this information may be useful in treating the injuries.

A Special Note about Cat Bites

Cats' mouths, especially, carry a lot of bacteria, so any time a tooth breaks the skin, infection is a possibility. People whose immune systems are compromised, whether they have an infection or the HIV virus, are more likely to develop complications from a cat bite, *but even fully healthy individuals should take extra care with a cat bite.* The puncture nature of a cat bite (dog bites tend to be more of a flesh *tear*) makes the wound both difficult to clean and highly susceptible to infection that can even lead to amputation in severe circumstances. If it's a very superficial wound, clean it well with running water for 10 to 15 minutes and use an antibacterial soap. Be sure you actually clean the wound. Just pouring on alcohol does not clean it, and in the words of our veterinary expert reviewer, "Pouring alcohol on the wound would burn like hell!" He further advises to apply over-the-counter triple antibiotic ointment or Betadine ointment to the wound, if possible, before seeking treatment.

Promptly seek medical attention for any bite or scratch wound that is deep, reddened, swollen, painful, or draining. Your physician may recommend a round of antibiotics and a tetanus shot if yours is not current. That may sound like a hassle, but it beats losing your hand.

WHO IS BITING WHOM?

A study in El Paso, Texas, reviewed a random sample of dog and cat bites and found the following:

• 89.4 percent of cat bites were provoked, and the victims were mostly female (57.5 percent) and adult (68.3 percent).

• 44.6 percent of dog bites were provoked, and the victims were more likely to be male (65.6 percent) and children (63 percent).

These results likely indicate ownership and interaction patterns more than they do gender or age "bite preference" for the animals involved, but they do indicate that dogs frequently bite without obvious provocation, and that young boys should be taught to behave with sensitivity for their own well-being (and just to be nice).

Cat Scratch Fever

Cat scratch fever is a bacterial infection that can cause painful swelling in the lymph nodes, fatigue, headache, joint pain, seizures, and other symptoms. It is caused by *Rochalimaea henselae*, a bacillus picked up in the soil. It appears to be mainly transmitted by a bite or scratch from kittens, although mature cats and occasionally dogs will transmit the disease. Persons with compromised immune systems are more likely to have an adverse reaction. Certainly, not all cat scratches are of concern, and cat scratch fever generally goes away on its own after two to four weeks with lymph node symptoms. If necessary, it can be treated with antibiotics.

Dog-Bite-Related Fatalities

Dog-bite-related fatalities are extremely rare. The National Canine Research Council has a count of 33 such incidents nationwide in 2010, defined as a fatality where a human being died as a result of trauma, blood loss, or tearing of body parts. The overwhelming majority of dogs involved in these incidents were not family pets. Many were victims of abuse and neglect. "Pit-bull types" accounted for 23 of these attacks; rottweilers accounted for 4. The remaining breeds included: Siberian husky, American bulldog, mixed breed, bullmastiff, wolf-dog hybrid, boxer, and German shepherd.

Keep in mind that even if breed-specific bite rates could be accurately calculated, they do not factor in owner-related issues. For example, less responsible owners, or owners who want to foster aggression in their dogs, may be drawn differentially to certain breeds.

Another study indicates that dog bites that required medical attention were more likely to be caused by unneutered, chained, male dogs.

{ mammals }

This is another reminder to weigh carefully the needs and abilities of owners and prospective pets, as well as yet another reason to neuter animals that are not part of a purebred breeding effort.

The short interpretation is that, yes, pit bulls and rottweilers need to be watched closely, to be sure, but many other breeds under various conditions can be lethally dangerous as well. In the final analysis, it again comes down to us to treat animals with the care they need and the respect they deserve—for their safety and ours.

WILD ANIMAL ENCOUNTERS

Breaking and entering isn't just for human beings anymore. An 80-year-old widow in Washington Township, Ohio, was startled when a rambunctious deer smashed through her living room picture window. She fled out the front door, and she later admitted she "must have held the door open for him, because he bounded out the front door," too. Even that story pales before another incident in Jeffersonville, Kentucky, when a manic deer crashed through a school window to terrorize a roomful of kindergartners:

> They screamed as the deer broke a large window pane and bounded over tables, ran to a sink in the back of the classroom, leaped over a counter, and smashed into the blackboard, before breaking two more windows on its way out, about a minute later. . . . The deer injured itself when it crashed through the window and hit the blackboard, leaving a large bloody spot.

These cases may be bizarre, but they do illustrate that anything can happen with wildlife; that's why it's called "wild." Of course, these instances and the unusual events you can catch on TV are not the norm, but here are a few directions to reduce further your chances of a dangerous encounter.

Minimizing Wild Encounters

Common sense dictates these obvious guidelines:

- ☞ Animals will not generally attack unless provoked, starving, or ill. Provocation can include physical abuse, crowding, or frustrating

HEAVENLY HELP FOR ANIMAL ATTACKS

Pray to St. Vitus, the patron saint for the prevention of animal attacks, as well as the protector of actors, comedians, comediennes, Czechoslovakia (now the Czech Republic and Slovakia), dancers, dogs, epileptics, lightning, and storms. (I'm not making this stuff up.)

the creature (as when you entice it with edibles and then withhold the food).

☞ Do not corner or handle wild animals. Many wild animals cannot tolerate the stress of a human encounter. Your interference may cause their death or your injury.

☞ Do not approach young offspring when the elder animals are in attendance. (See "Aid to the Wounded or Abandoned" below.)

☞ Do not disturb a feeding animal, and give it and the surrounding territory a wide berth. You cannot know how much that meal may mean to the animal that may be quite ready to defend this essential component of life.

☞ Do not disturb animals that are mating. Among other things, it's stupid, discourteous, and potentially damaging to you, them, and their species in the long run.

☞ Do not separate fighting animals using your bare hands. If separation is really necessary—say, if your dog is tangling with a raccoon—drive the animals apart using a long stick or club while keeping a good distance from the heavy action. A loud noise such as a car horn may help to startle the animals apart.

Treatment for Animal Attacks

The basic field treatment for all animal bites and maulings is the same, regardless of the animal that may produce different types of wounds and risks of infection.

☞ Apply pressure to stop any brisk bleeding.

☞ Clean the wounds well by flushing all injuries that have broken the skin with at least two quarts of disinfected water, scrubbing with mild soap, and flushing again.

☞ If you are carrying povidone iodine (Betadine) solution 10 percent (not soap or scrub); benzalkonium chloride (Zephiran) liquid 1 percent antiseptic; or, in a pinch, Bactine antiseptic (benzalkonium 0.13 percent), rinse the wound with one of these for one minute (to help kill the rabies virus), then rinse away the solution until there is no discoloration of the wound.

☞ Unless it is absolutely essential for rescue, minimize the risk of infection by not sewing or taping closed any animal bite. If a large tear is present, the wound edges can be held together with tape and wraps. Apply a thin layer of antibacterial cream into the wound.

☞ If the victim is more than five hours from a physician, administer antibiotics. Especially if the bite is from a cat, administer an antibiotic as soon as possible.

{ mammals }

15

Aid to the Wounded or Abandoned

Encounters with injured or potentially abandoned wildlife are a part of modern life for most people. It can be heart wrenching trying to determine what to do, and your choices may put you at risk, depending on the species and the circumstances. You should leave larger wounded wild mammals, such as raccoons and opossums, to the wildlife care experts. *Do not attempt to capture them yourself.*

You should almost always secure professionally trained care for any animal you do rescue by transporting it yourself to a facility or by summoning wildlife personnel while you isolate or watch the whereabouts of the creature.

Professional care is almost always a must for several reasons:

☞ It is illegal for individuals to possess or treat wildlife without a permit issued by appropriate state or federal agencies. While not illegal under Ohio law at the time of the incident in October 2011, the tragedy of nonprofessionals keeping exotic animals was forced into the national spotlight when owner Terry Thompson released his wild menagerie in Zanesville, Ohio, and then took his own life. Only a few of his creatures survived. Forty-eight—including 12 lions, 8 bears, and 18 endangered Bengal tigers—were gunned down in the name of public safety. Thompson had previously been convicted of animal abuse. The fact that Ohio has some of the most lax laws in the nation on the keeping of exotics further ignited the political debate.

☞ Professionals can administer the proper diet as well as care. Unsuitable diet and handling can often lead to unnecessary fatalities.

☞ Through a lack of knowledge and proper equipment, you may expose yourself and your family to disease.

If you have found a wild animal that you think is injured or orphaned, immediately call one of the following resources for assistance. Most can be located fairly easily through your local telephone directory or online.

☞ A local wildlife rehabilitator
☞ A local animal shelter
☞ A local animal control agency
☞ A local wildlife/exotic animals veterinarian
☞ A local nature center
☞ A local wild bird store
☞ A state wildlife management agency

Describe the animal and its physical condition as accurately as possible and carefully follow the instructions you are given. Signs that a wild animal needs help:

- Bleeding
- Vomiting
- Shivering
- Evidence of a dead parent nearby
- A featherless or nearly featherless bird (nestling) on the ground
- A wild animal presented to you by a cat or dog
- An apparently or obviously broken limb

Many animals that appear to be orphaned are not. Here are some tips to help you know when not to rescue a baby animal. Unless one or more of the signs mentioned above is present, *do not attempt to rescue an animal in any of the following circumstances*:

- A fawn curled up in grass and approachable—its mother most likely out of sight but nearby and watching you.
- A bird that is feathered with some downy tufts and is hopping on the ground but unable to fly—it is a fledgling and its parents are probably nearby.
- A rabbit that is 4 inches long with open eyes and erect ears—it is independent.
- An opossum that is 7 inches or longer (not including the tail)—it is independent.
- A squirrel that is small but fully furred and able to climb—it is a juvenile but independent.

OPOSSUMS AND RACCOONS

These two critters are so commonly found around human dwellings that they bear mentioning. Odds are good that if you have these nighttime ramblers poking about your environs, you'll have no safety issues if you don't engage or threaten them.

Of course, the opossum is the one that looks like the biggest rat you have ever seen. They're roughly the size of house cats and top out at about 15 pounds. Opossums are primitive animals that date back to the dinosaur age, which is remarkable because they are notoriously dimwitted. But, hey, survival of the species is the bottom line, and they are great at it even if they also have a high mortality rate at all stages of life and only live for about three years. What makes us interested in them is that they have 50 sharp teeth, more than any other mammal. When they are threatened, sometimes they feign death by "playing possum," a proven defense even against the jaws of a Siberian husky inside a fenced yard.

However, the *National Audubon Society Field Guide to North American Mammals* describes this vivid alternative opossum behavior: "More often,

{ mammals }

OPOSSUM

it tries to bluff its attacker by hissing, screeching, salivating, opening its mouth wide to show all of its 50 teeth, and sometimes excreting a greenish substance." It can also emit smelly stuff from its anal glands. So, if you find a possum in your garage ransacking your pet food (they eat just about anything, which is why they continue to thrive), don't get in there and start whacking away with the broom, trying to corner or to capture it. The very fine book, *Living with Wildlife: How to Enjoy, Cope with, and Protect North America's Wild Creatures Around Your Home and Theirs,* recommends that you "use bright lights, make loud noises by banging pans, rustling paper, opening/closing doors, or playing radios; and/or squirting water to frighten them away." After the opossum leaves, take better care to store your edibles more securely. Another potential troubling situation might arise with a female that is trying to defend her young, so fully assess any situation to the best of your ability.

Raccoons, of course, are the masked bandits that are quite, quite clever, as well as exceptionally dexterous. They can grow to more than three feet in length and weigh up to almost 50 pounds. Television ads that show them entering a house by turning the doorknob and then opening the refrigerator to raid for snacks before flopping on the sofa are not that far-fetched. According to *Living with Wildlife*, if you find a raccoon in your house, close the doors to other rooms and open all the windows and doors you can to give the raccoon an easy exit. Don't try to lure it out with food, as this will reinforce the food association that might prompt the raccoon to return.

Alarmed and anxious raccoons can cause extensive damage. If the animal doesn't leave in a reasonable amount of time, then call the local

Opossum (Virginia opossum)

- The opossum can bite if cornered.
- Up to 40 inches in length, including a 10–20 inch prehensile, hairless tail. Weighs up to 14 pounds.
- About the size of a house cat, the opossum has silvery "grizzled" hairs covering black hairs below. Its pinkish nose is long and pointed.
- This marsupial, unique to North America, has no comparable cousin.
- Omnivorous, the opossum eats insects, small mammals, bird eggs, grain, fruit, and carrion.
- Opossum litters, produced two or three times a year, are comprised of tiny young with up to 14 members—each about the size of a honeybee.
- Opossums are found in suburban areas, farmlands, and forests, usually near water.
- They are generally not aggressive but will defend themselves if cornered. They are nocturnal and solitary, and they are often killed on the highway as they attempt to feed on carrion.

wildlife authorities. Don't try to handle the animal yourself. Raccoons are strong, and they have sharp teeth and claws. Warning signs of an aggressive raccoon include growling, snarling, hissing, a lowered head with flattened ears, bared teeth, and bushed-out neck and shoulder fur. (You probably could've guessed that, right?)

Raccoons are formidable, and most predators know that to engage one can mean a losing fight to the death. A raccoon, for example, can dispatch a single dog, which is probably why coon hunters use packs of dogs in their pursuit. Raccoons, however, are not normally aggressive animals unless they are cornered, mating, or with young. They do carry a roundworm, *Baylisascaris procyonis*, in their dung. While not harmful to the raccoon, this organism is potentially very injurious to other mammals, including humans. For this reason, and also because the raccoon is a rabies carrier, it is unwise to entice these admittedly charming creatures with food.

Thwarting Opossums and Raccoons

☛ Do not leave pet food or trash outdoors at night. Contain your compost pile.

{ mammals }

RACCOON

Common Raccoon (Procyon lotor)

- The raccoon can bite if cornered. Because the animal can be a carrier of rabies, the bite is potentially fatal.
- It is common throughout the lower 48 states, with the exception pockets of the Rockies and pockets of the southwestern U.S.
- Up to 37 inches in length, including a tail of 8 to 16 inches.
- The raccoon is distinguished by its black mask and black-ringed tail on a grayish-brown body. It has a pointed snout.
- The raccoon's omnivorous diet includes grain, nuts, berries, rodents, insects, crayfish, bird eggs, and carrion.
- One litter per year of usually four young is delivered in the spring.
- The raccoon is highly adapted in suburban areas, and is also found near water in forests, bottomlands, and in rocky outcroppings.
- Nocturnal, curious, and extremely dexterous, the raccoon is not aggressive but will fight ferociously if cornered or to defend itself.

- Pick fruit and garden crops when they are ripe, and do not leave rotten fruit or crops on the ground.
- Eliminate brush piles, dilapidated buildings, and holes under concrete slabs.
- Raccoons, opossums, and skunks (!) will easily enter a house through the pet door, so secure them at night.

For more solutions to various scenarios involving these backyard buddies, consult *Living with Wildlife: How to Enjoy, Cope with, and Protect North America's Wild Creatures Around Your Home and Theirs* by the California Center for Wildlife with Diana Landau and Shelley Stump.

SKUNKS

Everybody thinks of skunks first when they think of an odoriferous encounter, and certainly they are the species most likely to let their "love" linger on you or your pet. There are other mammals of the same *Mustelidae* family you are much less likely to encounter who can also "let it fly," such as badgers, minks, and weasels. For some of these species, the scent release is a form of marking and sexual attraction rather than defense, but a skunk's spray speaks clearly, saying, "Stay away!"

Skunks of one kind or another are found throughout the U.S., with the striped skunk the one most commonly encountered. Skunks only spray when threatened; there are several accounts of peaceful coexistence between skunks and humans. It is true that de-scented skunks (this must be done at a very early age) make good pets, behaving similarly to cats. In the wild, though, the skunk you or your dog encounters will likely initiate defensive action rather quickly. Even so, skunks will probably first demonstrate the following behaviors before they send the spray (which is not urine) at you or Fido.

Warning Signs before a Skunk Sprays
- Bushing out its fur.
- Shaking its tail.
- Stamping the ground with its forefeet.
- Growling.
- Turning its head and spitting.

If a skunk turns its body into a U-shape or does a handstand (no kidding), run, run, run away. If a skunk aims its anus at you, get ready to dodge a 15-foot fan-patterned spray fired with precision accuracy. Skunks have teeth, and they can bite, but they rarely need to use them, so effective is their special formula.

{ mammals }

21

A skunk's special formula is a yellow oil composed of thiols and thio-acetate derivatives of these thiols, a substance stored in two walnut-sized glands with openings in the anus. Generally, a skunk can store enough for about five to six sprays, but because replenishment takes time, skunks are judicious about the spray and only fire when they feel they really need to. The human nose can detect skunk spray thiols at about 10 parts per billion, and anybody who has driven country roads with open windows knows it is a unique and powerful scent. It is so powerful and long-lasting, in fact, that the offending elements are chemically removed and the remaining substance is used in perfume manufacture.

De-Skunking Pets: The Myth of Tomato Juice

Bonnie was a nosy dog that was "skunked" more than once. The first time, the spray was administered at such close range Bonnie's white face fur was yellow. She received a good blast in the eyes, but seemed to have no blindness, temporary or otherwise. Flushing her face with water from a garden hose to reduce the concentration in her eyes was the first order of business. Next came the tomato juice treatment, which some people swear by. I thought it was just a messy failure.

William F. Wood of the Department of Chemistry at Humboldt State University agrees.

> *Bathing an animal in tomato juice seems to work because at high doses of skunk spray, the human nose quits smelling the odor (olfactory fatigue). When this happens, the odor of tomato*

SKUNK

Striped Skunk (Mephitis mephitis)

- The main hazard skunks pose is spraying, but a bite is potentially fatal, as the animal is a carrier of rabies.
- These skunks are common throughout the U.S. with the exception of the southern tip of Florida and a small corner of the southwestern U.S.
- Up to 31 inches in length, including a tail of 5 to 9 inches.
- They are black with two broad white stripes that begin as a cap on the head and run the length of the upper body and down the tail.
- The spotted skunk has more mottled black and white markings.
- The skunk is omnivorous, eating berries, insects, grubs, bird eggs, amphibians, and small mammals.
- Breeding occurs February to April with litters of four to seven born in May.
- Skunks are found in suburbs, forests, grasses, and desert lands.
- Mother skunk is extremely protective of her young and will spray to defend. Both sexes generally give warning postures before powerful, foul-smelling, long-lasting spray is released.

juice can easily be detected. A person suffering olfactory fatigue to skunk spray will swear that the skunk odor is gone and was neutralized by the tomato juice. Another person coming on the scene at this point will readily confirm that the skunk spray has not been neutralized by the tomato juice. To neutralize or deodorize skunk spray, the chemicals in the secretion must be changed to a different type of molecule. Tomato juice does not work.

Another chemist, Paul Krebaum, concocted these chemically based "antidotes" to skunk spray:

Be careful not to get this solution in your pet's eyes.

For pets that have been sprayed, bathe them in a mixture of:
- ☛ 1 quart of 3 percent hydrogen peroxide (from drug store)
- ☛ ¼ cup of baking soda (sodium bicarbonate) and
- ☛ 1 teaspoon of liquid detergent.

After five minutes, rinse the animal with water. Repeat if necessary. The mixture must be used immediately and will not work if it is stored for any length of time. Do not store in a closed container. The oxygen

{ mammals }

gas that forms could break the container. Note: This mixture may bleach the pet's hair. Rumor has it that a black Labrador became a chocolate after her de-skunking treatment, but since fur grows out, the interval of a pleasant-smelling pet seems a small price to pay.

Skunk Spray on Your Clothers and Clean-up Towels and Rags

After conducting this pet treatment outside to prevent odor contamination in your house, wash your clothes and/or rags sullied in this procedure with one cup of liquid laundry bleach per gallon of water.

Skunk Spray on Buildings and Decks

To sanitize the exterior of buildings, deck surfaces, etc., apply a solution of liquid laundry bleach, such as Clorox, (one cup per gallon). Caution: This may bleach the surface, so try it first on a small area if colorfastness could be a problem. The bleach must come in contact with the spot where the secretion was sprayed. Repeated applications may be necessary for large amounts of the skunk spray. Do not use this solution on pets.

Skunk Spray over a Large Area or Trapped in a House

Time and adequate ventilation alone will help. Sorry!

Minimizing Skunk Encounters

Beyond the spray factor, skunks are carriers of rabies. Here are some suggestions for discouraging their presence:

- ☞ Do not feed the skunks.
- ☞ Do not leave pet food outside or discard edible garbage skunks can access. This includes compost piles.
- ☞ Secure garbage containers.
- ☞ Keep pet doors closed at night to prevent illegal entry by a skunk.
- ☞ Keep fruit trees picked and do not leave rotted fruit on the ground.
- ☞ Skunks are attracted to birdseed and to the birds and rodents that use the feeder.
- ☞ If possible, eliminate outdoor sources of water.
- ☞ If a skunk wanders into your garage, leave an outside door open and let the skunk leave in its own good time.
- ☞ Securely enclose chickens, especially at night, making sure the fencing has no holes and that it extends 6 to 8 inches underground to prevent skunks and other animals from digging under.
- ☞ To eliminate suitable nesting cavities, remove debris and brush piles or at least stack them neatly.

Living with Wildlife: How to Enjoy, Cope with, and Protect North America's Wild Creatures Around Your Home and Theirs by the California Center for Wildlife with Diana Landau and Shelley Stump and Bill Adler, Jr.'s *Outwitting Critters: A Human Guide for Confronting Devious Animals and Winning* are good resources for solutions to other skunk-related problems, such as when skunks want to live under your house.

COYOTES

> *Coyotes are unique among urban wildlife in that they are often considered a nuisance before any damage occurs; simply their presence alone is considered a nuisance. People are uncomfortable with the idea that a relatively large predator is living near them, regardless of any signs of conflict.*
>
> —The Cook County, Illinois, Coyote Project

FAMILY TIES

Coyotes are among the most adaptable mammals in North America. Some live alone, others in mated pairs, and others in packs, which may consist of one mated pair, their new young, and offspring from the previous season that have not yet left their parents. Packs have the natural advantages for hunting and defense.

"Ghost Dog" A.K.A "The Trickster"

Coyotes hold a very important place in mythology and folklore. Identified as "the trickster," that part of life that makes us laugh at ourselves or forces us into new solutions as old and outdated ideas crumble, the mythological coyote is inventive, mischievous, and evasive.

Mythological coyote (Both pronunciations, ky-ote and ky-o-tee, are acceptable) has been compared to both the Scandinavian Loki, and also Prometheus, who shared with Coyote the trick of having stolen fire from the gods as a gift for mankind, and Anansi, a mythological culture hero from Western African mythology. French anthropologist Claude Lévi-Strauss proposed a theory that Coyote (and Crow) obtained mythic status because they are mediator animals between life and death and because they have a contradictory and unpredictable personality.

Coexistence with a fairly large, unpredictable, wild creature makes many of us uncomfortable. Coyotes presently challenge us to reappraise the realities of wild and local danger in our neighborhoods. Seeing a coyote in your yard can trigger a powerful feral response, an "us versus them" adrenaline rush that urges us to "do something." As we'll see,

{ mammals }

that "do something" is not killing coyotes on sight. It's educating our-selves on how to avoid difficult and unwanted encounters.

Sometimes called "God's Dog," "Ghost Dog," "Brush Dog," or "Song Dog," coyotes are with us to stay. They inhabit most of North America and all of the lower 48 states. Extremely clever and adaptive, our beloved dogs' "cousins" demand our respect because we are not going to exterminate them. Nor would we want to.

More Rats Than Cats

Like most humans, coyotes are opportunistic omnivores. Based on the contents of 1,429 scats collected during 2000–2002, the Cook County, Illinois, study determined a typical coyote diet for that area.

- Small rodents 42%
- White-tailed deer 22%
- Fruit 23%
- Eastern cottontail 18%
- Bird 13%
- Raccoon 8%
- Grass 6%
- Invertebrates 4%
- Human-associated 2% *(garbage, etc.)*
- Muskrat 1%
- Domestic cat 1%
- Unknown 1%

The Cook County report continued, "As we have seen, rodents make up the bulk of the coyote diet in both urban areas and rural areas. Although it has yet to be measured in urban systems, experiments in rural areas have shown that the removal of coyotes results in a dramatic increase in rodent abundance. . . . We have observed rodent increases in areas such as golf courses following coyote removal programs. There

FROM THE COOK COUNTY STUDY:

We were surprised to find so many coyotes living near people in Cook County, and yet relatively few conflicts have been reported.

We assumed that with an average of 350 coyotes removed each year from the area as nuisances, most urban coyotes would create problems. In contrast, only five of 175 radio-collared coyotes have been removed as nuisances (as defined by the local community). Apparently, few coyotes have become nuisances in Cook County, and it is likely that this is true of other metropolitan areas. It remains to be seen if conflicts will remain relatively rare or if they become more common as coyotes adjust to living with humans.

For perspective, it is worth considering that no documented case of a coyote biting a human has been reported for Cook County. Contrast that result with domestic dogs, in which Cook County often records 2,000 to 3,000 dog bites each year (in-cluding some fatalities). In 2005, there were no recorded bites on people by coyotes in Cook County, but 3,043 bites were recorded for domestic dogs (data from Cook County Animal and Rabies Control).

COYOTE

is also the possibility that coyotes help to control woodchucks. Many areas, such as cemeteries and golf courses, have reported declines in woodchuck abundance once coyotes appeared."

Deer are often overabundant and difficult to manage in urban areas. Although coyotes rarely take adult deer, they are primary predators of deer fawns. An Illinois Natural History Survey conducted a fawn survival study in different locations within the Chicago area and found that coyotes killed 20 percent to 80 percent of the fawns in different populations. Coyotes cannot reduce deer populations because they do not often take adult deer (in the Midwest), but they may slow population growth in high-density areas through their predation on fawns.

Canada geese have adapted to urban landscapes much like deer and at times become overabundant and a nuisance. Studies confirm that population growth is limited by nest predation, primarily by coyotes. As with deer, coyotes do not take enough adult geese to reduce the population, but they can slow the population increase through egg predation.

Tips and Tools for Keeping Coyotes Wild

Project Coyote, a California-based organization that promotes peaceful coexistence with coyotes, and the Humane Society of the United States offer this advice on how to discourage coyotes from coming into urban areas:

- ☛ Do not feed coyotes.
- ☛ Keep your pet on a leash.
- ☛ Supervise small pets and children, and keep your cats indoors.

{ mammals }

- If you have dogs that spend time in your fenced yard, you may want to invest in a Coyote Roller, a device that attaches to the top of a fence to stop coyote paws from getting a grip. Also, adding 6 inches of wire mesh to the bottom of your fence should deter coyotes from digging underneath.
- Keep garbage, compost, and pet food out of reach. Make sure your garbage can lids are on tight, and feed your cats and dogs indoors.
- If faced with a coyote, act big and loud—shake a can of pennies, blow a whistle, wave your arms above your head. Such actions will reinforce their fear of humans, which is good for us and them.
- Ask your neighbors to follow the above tips, too.
- Statistically, lightning, cows, and deer pose a greater personal threat than coyotes. However, if you are concerned about coyotes and go walking in the woods alone, stay alert, and leave your portable audio device at home so you can be aware of your surroundings.

Tragedies

The Road Runner always gets the best of him in the Warner Brothers classic cartoons, but what about our chances when it comes to coyotes? Small mammals including pet cats do "disappear" where coyotes are prevalent, but fatal attacks on humans are very rare. There are two documented cases.

One was a 3-year-old girl in Glendale, California, in the 1980s. Her family had a habit of leaving food for coyotes and then observing them from lawn chairs while the coyotes ate. Had the family not engaged the feral animals, it is likely this tragedy could have been avoided. Humans must acknowledge their part in these tragic wild encounters.

The second case is that of a 19-year-old folk singer from Toronto who died in 2009 after being attacked by two coyotes in Cape Breton Highlands National Park in Nova Scotia. Taylor Josephine Stephanie Luciow, who went by the stage name Taylor Mitchell, was hiking alone on a popular trail when she was attacked. Retired Department of Natural Resources biologist Bob Bancroft said this kind of attack is extremely rare and that he had never heard of such a serious case in Nova Scotia. Bancroft continued, "Coyotes, which are normally up to 50 pounds, are usually very shy, although they can be bold. . . . In situations like a national park [where] usually there's no hunting and no trapping allowed, they can get used to a human presence and not have much fear of any retribution. . . . Coyotes team up to take down deer, and it's possible the hiker didn't even realize what was happening. They may have snuck up on her and

FRIGHTEN COYOTES

Coyotes are disturbed by noise. Even yelling and clapping from a hundred yards away can discourage them. If you have a large population of coyotes near you, consider making one or both of these deterrent tools described on nashvillecoyotes.com. (This site has extensive information and was highly useful in the preparation of these pages.)

THE CAN CLANGER
Materials:
- Five or six empty tin cans
- A can opener
- A piece of strong string or rope

Remove the labels from the tins and make a small hole in each tin with the can opener. Thread the string through the tins, and then tie the two ends of the string together. Use the clang whenever a coyote uses your yard to feed or rest. Walk toward the coyote, appearing as aggressive as possible. Shake or throw the can clanger at the coyote while shouting in a deep low voice. Several adults appear more threatening than one. Each adult should carry a different deterrent (for example, a hockey stick, broom, can clanger, basketball) and use it to chase the coyote from the area. Don't stop at your property line because a coyote in your neighbor's yard poses just as much threat as one in your own. Teach coyotes to avoid areas of human activity.

COYOTE SHAKER
Materials:
- Soda or juice can
- Aluminum foil
- About 40 pennies
- Duct tape

Place the pennies in the can and cover the opening with tape. Cut a piece of foil and tape it around the can. Shake the tin at the coyote. The shaker scares the approaching coyote through aggressive hand motion, loud noise, and reflective light. This tool can fit in a pocket or bag.

knocked her over before she even knew what happened. They may have been youngsters. They just may not have had a lot of experience, or they may have just capitalized on a situation where a young person was acting vulnerable and very frightened by their presence.

If a Coyote Approaches You
- ☞ Be aggressive yourself by waving your arms, stomping and yelling loudly in a deep voice. Appear as large and threatening as possible. Coyotes are naturally timid animals and will flee when confronted with aggression.
- ☞ Stand your ground and stare it in the eye. Never run away. It is more likely to consider you prey, give chase, and seriously harm you.

{ mammals }

☞ Be prepared: The best defense is a good offence; carry a whistle, flashlight, and/or personal alarm. This is especially important for small children who play outside or walk to school in areas where coyotes have been spotted.

☞ Stay together: If you are walking in an area that has high coyote activity, never do so without a companion.

☞ Don't lure them with food: Coyotes are scavengers. If you have pets, feed them inside the house rather than leaving food outside. Don't leave meat scraps or products in compost buckets outside your house; keep regular compost in an enclosed area and ensure garbage bins have tight resealable lids to keep out animals.

If the Coyote Keeps Approaching You

☞ Continue to exaggerate the techniques listed above.

☞ Do not turn away or run.

☞ Maintain eye contact and move slowly toward a building or area of increased activity.

Coyote Skill Set

☞ Coyotes are good swimmers and can run up to 40 mph.

☞ They can jump distances up to 13 feet.

☞ They can snatch a pet running off leash in an instant and can bite through extended retractable leashes.

☞ They are skillful hunters that sometimes work in pairs.

☞ They are most active from dusk to dawn.

☞ They do not appreciate boundaries and often grab pets that walk near woods.

☞ They are attracted to easy food sources, but eat just about anything, so they don't depend on humans for food. This means they are not compelled to be around humans who are taking good precautions.

Don't Attract Coyotes—Deter Them!

The Colorado Division of Wildlife developed this home audit list:

☞ Never intentionally feed wildlife!

☞ Never feed pets outside and store all pet foods inside.

☞ Remove pet bowls, birdbaths, fountains, and ponds, particularly those containing fish.

☞ Place feeders where only birds can reach them.

☞ Remove bird feeders or clean up seed dropped on the ground to reduce the presence of small mammals.

☞ Clean up fruit that has fallen on the ground from trees and shrubs.

☞ Fully enclose gardens and compost piles.

- Burn food off of BBQ grills and clean after each use.
- Secure all trash containers with locking lids. Periodically clean cans to reduce residual odors.
- Trim vegetation to reduce hiding places.
- Restrict access under decks, around woodpiles, or any structure that can provide cover.
- A 6-foot high fence with top rollers can deter coyotes from entering portions of your property. Check local building codes.
- Always supervise your pets when outside, especially dusk through dawn and during the mating and pup rearing periods of January through June.
- Fully enclose outdoor pet kennels.
- Walk pets on a 6-foot leash.

How Can I Keep My Animals Safe?

- The only way to ensure your cat is safe from coyotes is to keep it indoors.
- If cats do go outside, bring them in at dusk.
- You may need to give your cat outdoors time by building an enclosed cat run.
- Sometimes coyotes do prey upon small dogs and have even taken dogs directly off the leash.
- Supervise your dog it at all times when outside.
- Allow your dog off-leash only in enclosed areas.
- If you encounter a coyote while walking your dog, gather your dog in your arms.
- If this is not possible, keep it on a short leash as you move toward an area with increased activity.
- Again, shout, wave your arms, or throw objects at the coyote.
- Large dogs rarely come into conflict with coyotes. Incidents generally occur during the late winter and early spring when coyotes mate and are more territorial. Do not let your dog play or interact with coyotes.
- Keep a whistle handy while walking your dog. The whistle may not scare the coyote directly (coyotes hear the same sirens, car alarms, and horns as we do), but it will alert other pedestrians in the area of your need for help.
- Walk your dog in areas of high pedestrian traffic such as busy streets and jogging and park trails. Walk during times of increased activity such as during daylight hours, around schools at arrival, dismissal, break, or lunch periods; along transit routes as the work day begins or ends; and around parks when sporting events (for example, soccer practice) are being held.

{ mammals }

Coyote (Canis latrans)

- Coyotes are a lethal threat to small companion animals such as cats and small dogs, plus livestock such as sheep.
- They are common throughout Northern America.
- Roughly 4 feet in body length, they have bushy tails roughly 15 inches long. They weigh 20 to 45 pounds. Size and weight vary by range, with the heavier animals generally east of the Mississippi.
- A medium-sized canine with the shaggy coat of a wolf and the sharp face of a fox, the color of the coyote's pelt varies from grayish-brown to yellowish-gray on the upper parts, while the throat and belly tend to be buff or white. The forelegs, sides of the head, muzzle, and paws are reddish-brown. The back has tawny-colored under-fur and long, black-tipped guard hairs that form a black dorsal stripe and a dark cross on the shoulder area. Fur color varies by region.
- Omnivorous and opportunistic, the coyote prefers fresh meat and fruit, but will eat carrion, insects, bird eggs, and grain plus human garbage, birdseed, and grass.
- Litter size ranges from one to 19 pups; the average is six. Large litters act as a compensatory measure against the high juvenile mortality rate. About 50–70 percent of pups do not survive to adulthood.
- Coyotes have adapted to urban and suburban areas, as well as farmlands and forests.
- Coyotes are highly adaptable animals. Shy, they can be frightened easily. They are generally nocturnal and may hunt solo, in pairs, or with a pack of five to six. Filling the food-chain niche once held by wolves, "the tricksters" are here to stay.

☞ Walk your dog with friends and family.
☞ Avoid walking along abandoned properties or densely vegetated areas.
☞ Make sure your dog is ahead of you and within sight at all times while walking.
☞ Any dog that is off leash should have an immediate and totally trustworthy recall response to eliminate potential conflict with coyotes, dogs, and people.

Prepare Your Children for Potential Coyote Encounters

Education prior to an encounter is key. Teach children to:

- ☞ Never Run.
- ☞ Be Big (stand up and raise your arms in the air).
- ☞ Be Mean (sound angry, stomp your feet, and throw something at the coyote).
- ☞ Be Loud (yelling "Go away, coyote!" so people nearby will come help).

If You Find an Injured, Sick, or Abandoned Coyote Pup

People often see coyote pups and other wildlife babies alone in the spring. Before the animal is approached, it should first be observed for at least 24 hours to ensure the parent is not returning to take care of its young. If you are certain it is orphaned contact your nearest wildlife rehabilitation centre. Pest control companies are likely to kill the animal.

Do not attempt to handle an adult coyote. Injured wild animals are frightened and in pain. In addition, adult coyotes are extremely difficult to catch so long as they have use of all four limbs. Call the City of Chicago Animal Control and Rescue. In limited emergency circumstances they may provide traps and pick up the captured animals. Call 311 for assistance. You may also consult the Web page Living with Wildlife in Illinois (http://web.extension.illinois.edu/wildlife/). It lists many specific options for rehabilitators.

Coyote-Dog Hybrids

People often speculate as to the frequency of "coydogs" in urban settings. Coyotes and dogs are related, and they are biologically capable of producing hybrid litters. Coydogs have been raised in captivity. Genetic surveys of coyotes have rarely documented evidence of dogs in the genetic makeup of coyotes, despite domestic dogs and coyotes sharing the continent for the past 9,000 years. Although it is possible, coydogs in urban settings are unlikely because:

- ☞ Coyotes are highly seasonal breeders; dogs are not.
- ☞ Coydog females have a shifted estrus cycle that does not coincide with the coyote period.
- ☞ Domestic dog and coydog males do not tend to litters, whereas male coyotes do.
- ☞ Coydogs may have lower fertility than either domestic dogs or coyotes.

(Thanks again to nashvillecoyotes.com—an excellent national resource.)

{ mammals }

33

BATS
The Bat Rap

Bats !
Bats go flying in the night,
Some give people a lot of fright,
Most people think they're very scary,
But most of them are just cute and hairy!
—By students Chelsea Reber and Hannah Hansen

From rain forests to deserts, bats play key roles in ecosystems around the globe, especially by eating insects, including agricultural pests. Some experts estimated that one bat can eat between 600 to 1,000 insects, mosquitoes included, within a period of one hour. In rural and urban settings bats can be observed at twilight, dipping and circling in a "loopy" flight pattern that resembles that of a butterfly more than a bird.

In a given group of bat watchers, perhaps for lack of something more interesting to say, almost invariably someone will pronounce, "Bats carry rabies, you know." This is a true statement, but one that still requires a sense of proportion. Your risk of exposure is truly tiny, but if you do contract rabies from a bat, you may not know it until it is too late. For this reason and because bats are small enough to enter your house without your immediate knowledge, we will devote several pages to this animal's capacity to transmit rabies. You should not construe this coverage to mean that all bats are dangerous. This is simply not true, and this false notion can deprive you of the pleasure of simply observing them in the wild.

Frequency of Rabies

Each year, scientists from the Centers for Disease Control and Prevention (CDCP) collect information about cases of animal and human rabies from the state health departments and publish the information in a summary report. In the last hundred years or so, rabies fatalities have declined from about 100 annually to 2 or 3. In data collected from 1995 to 2011, none of these fatalities were in Illinois.

Wild Animals? No. Bats? Yes.

Wild animals accounted for 92 percent of reported cases of rabies in the most recent data. Raccoons continued to be the most frequently reported rabid wildlife species (36.5 percent of all animal cases), followed by skunks (23.5 percent), bats (23.2 percent), foxes (7.0 percent), and other wild animals, including rodents and lagomorphs (1.8

percent). Reported cases decreased among all wild animals. The Chicago area, fortunately, is not at risk for the so-called wild terrestrial species named above. If you are going to contract rabies from a wild animal, it almost certainly will be from a bat.

Magic Bat Bites

The reasons for the preponderance of human rabies cases associated with bats remain speculative, but findings suggest that rabies can be transmitted after minor, undetected exposures. Insectivorous bats such as those implicated in the human rabies deaths in the U.S. have small teeth that may not cause an obvious wound in human skin. For this reason it is important to treat persons for rabies exposure when the possibility of a bat bite cannot be reasonably excluded. In all cases where bat-human contact has occurred, the bat should be collected and tested for rabies if that scenario is both possible and safe. If the bat is not available for rabies testing, the need for a post-exposure prophylaxis (PEP), that is, intervening injections, should be assessed by public health officials familiar with recent recommendations and outbreaks in the area.

The modern rabies vaccine is safe and effective. Anyone who handles wild animals should obtain pre-exposure immunization, and anyone bitten or exposed to the saliva or nerve tissue of a suspected rabies-infected animal should immediately obtain post-exposure vaccination. This vaccination has been simplified and no longer requires a lengthy series of shots as it did in the past. Four shots are administered over a period of two weeks and are usually given in the upper arm.

Medical personnel should consider rabies as a diagnosis in any case presenting the acute onset and rapid progression of compatible

BROWN BAT

neurological signs, regardless of whether the patient reports a history of an animal bite. Although early diagnosis cannot save the patient, it may help minimize the number of other potential exposures and the subsequent need for PEP.

How Can I Tell If a Bat Has Rabies?

Rabies can be confirmed only in a laboratory. However, you should be suspicious of any bat that is:

- ☞ Active by day.
- ☞ Found in a place where bats are not usually seen, for example, in a room in your home or on the lawn.
- ☞ Unable to fly.
- ☞ Easily approached.

Bats such as these are far more likely than others to be rabid. Therefore, it is best never to handle any bat.

Children and "Injured or Orphaned" Bats

> Bats can see at night.
> But if a bat falls—don't touch.
> Bats hang upside down.

> —Bat Haiku by Quinn Franklin
> Third-grader in Arkansas

Children are instinctively drawn to animals, especially those within reach. They will also show concern for creatures they perceive to be orphaned or injured. Bats found on the ground are likely to be ill, perhaps from rabies. For this reason it is important to teach children what bats look like and not to approach or touch a bat lying on the ground.

What Should I Do If I Come in Contact with a Bat?

If you are bitten by a bat—or if infectious material, such as saliva or brain tissue, from a bat gets into your eyes, nose, mouth, or a wound—wash the affected area thoroughly and get medical advice immediately. Whenever both possible and safe, the bat should be captured and sent to a laboratory for rabies testing.

People usually know when they have been bitten by a bat, but, as we have stated, in rare cases they do not know because bats have small teeth that may leave marks that are not easily seen. In the following situations, the CDCP cautions you to seek medical advice and have the bat tested even in the absence of an obvious bite wound:

- ☞ If you awaken and find a bat in your room.
- ☞ See a bat in the room of an unattended child.

Big Brown Bat (Eptesicus fuscus)

- As applies to all species of bats, the Big Brown is a carrier of rabies that is contracted by humans chiefly through a bite or possibly through a cut, scratch, or mucous membrane that comes in contact with bat saliva or brains.
- Big Browns live in a wide range of habitats from farmlands and forests to Chicago neighborhoods and parks. Typical summer roosts are trees, snags, or man-made structures.
- They weigh .5–.75 ounce and have a wingspan of 13–16 inches. Females are slightly larger than males.
- Beetles make up most of their diet, but they also feed on corn rootworm, a serious agricultural pest, as well as mosquitoes.
- In early May through early June, Big Browns give birth to one pup in the western part of their range, and to twin pups in the eastern part of their range (including Chicago). After a gestation of 60 days, pups are born naked with eyes closed. Their eyes open in about 7 days and they will nurse for 32–40 days. Young start to fly in July and August and reach adult size by early September.
- They live roughly 19 years, with males usually outliving females.
- Highly social, roosting bats hang in tightly packed groups, and colonies can contain 5–500 individuals.
- Big Browns typically fly between 20–30 feet from the ground and have been recorded at speeds of 40 mph.
- Big Browns hibernate in winter and loose 25 percent of their body weight during hibernation. Hibernation places bats in a very vulnerable condition and if disturbed they could die. Let sleeping bats hang

In February 1995, the aunt of a 4-year-old girl was awakened by the sounds of a bat in the room where the child was sleeping. The child did not wake up until the bat was captured, killed, and discarded. The girl reported no bite, and no evidence of a bite wound was found when she was examined. One month later the child became sick and died of rabies. The dead bat was recovered from the yard and tested—it had rabies.

This tragic case demonstrates several points:

☞ This child's infection with rabies was most likely the result of a bat bite.

☞ Children sleep heavily and may not awaken from the presence of a small bat.

{ mammals }

☞ A bat bite can be superficial and not easily noticed.

☞ The bat was behaving abnormally. Instead of hiding, it was making unusual noises and was having difficulty flying. This strange behavior should have led to a strong suspicion of rabies.

☞ If the bat had been submitted for rabies testing, a positive test would have led to lifesaving anti-rabies treatment.

Remember, in situations in which a bat is physically present and you cannot reasonably rule out having been bitten, safely capture the bat for rabies testing and seek medical attention immediately.

When Are Bats Safe?

To repeat, most bats do not have rabies, especially those that are behaving normally, flying at dusk and dark. People cannot get rabies just from seeing a bat in an attic, in a cave, or at a distance. In addition, people cannot get rabies from having contact with bat guano (feces), blood, or urine, or from touching a bat on its fur, even though bats should never be handled!

You can also forget that urban folk tale about bats nesting in your beehive hairdo or dive-bombing your pompadour. It just "don't" happen unless you're "stylin'" with a head full of cucumber beetles.

What Should I Do If My Pet Is Exposed to a Bat?

If you think your pet or domestic animal has been bitten by a bat, contact a veterinarian or your health department for assistance immediately and have the animal tested for rabies. Keeping vaccinations current for cats, dogs, and other animals is the way to take the worry out of that scenario.

How Can I Keep Bats out of My Home?

Some bats live in buildings, and there may be no reason to evict them if there is little chance for contact with people. However, bats should always be prevented from entering rooms of your home. For assistance with "bat-proofing" your home, contact an animal control or wildlife conservation agency. If you choose to do the "bat-proofing" yourself:

☞ Carefully examine your home for holes that might allow bats entry into your living quarters. Any openings larger than a quarter-inch by a half-inch should be caulked.

☞ Use window screens, chimney caps, and draft-guards beneath doors to attics; fill electrical and plumbing holes with stainless steel wool or caulking; and ensure that all doors to the outside close tightly.

- Additional "bat-proofing" can prevent bats from roosting in attics or buildings by covering outside entry points.
- Observe where the bats exit at dusk and exclude them by loosely hanging clear plastic sheeting or bird netting over these areas so that bats can crawl out and leave, but cannot re-enter. After the bats have been excluded, the openings can be permanently sealed.
- Remember that during summer many young bats are unable to fly. If you exclude adult bats during this time, the young may be trapped inside and die or make their way into living quarters. Thus, if possible, avoid exclusion from May through August.
- Most bats leave in the fall or winter to hibernate so these are the best times to "bat-proof" your home.

For more information about "bat-proofing" your home and plenty of other excellent bat information, contact Bat Conservation International at www.batcon.org.

How Can I Safely Capture a Bat in My Home?

If a bat is present in your home and you cannot rule out the possibility of exposure, leave the bat alone and contact an animal control or public health agency for assistance. If professional help is unavailable, use precautions to capture the bat safely.

You will need:
- Leather work gloves
- Piece of cardboard
- Small box or coffee can
- Tape

When the bat lands, approach it slowly, while wearing the gloves, and place the box or coffee can over it. Slide the cardboard under the container to trap the bat inside. Tape the cardboard to the container securely and punch small air holes in the cardboard. Contact your health department or animal control authority to make arrangements for rabies testing.

If you see a bat in your home and you are sure no human or pet exposure has occurred, confine the bat to a room by closing all doors and windows leading out of the room except those to the outside. The bat will probably leave soon. If not, it can be caught as described, and released outdoors away from people and pets.

The answer is not to kill any bat you can. Many local populations of bats have been destroyed and many species are now endangered. This is a substantial loss to all, in part because bat studies have contributed to medical advances including the development of navigational aids for the blind.

{ mammals }

When people think about bats, they often imagine things that are not true. Bats are not blind, nor will they suck your blood—and most do not have rabies.

Preventing Bat-Transmitted Rabies

☞ Teach children never to handle unfamiliar animals, wild or domestic, even if they appear friendly. "Love your own, leave other animals alone" is a good principle for children to learn.

☞ Wash any wound from an animal thoroughly with soap and water and seek medical attention immediately.

☞ Have all dead, sick, or easily captured bats tested for rabies if exposure to people or pets occurs.

☞ Prevent bats from entering living quarters or occupied spaces in homes, churches, schools, and other areas where they might contact people and pets.

☞ Be a responsible pet owner by keeping vaccinations current for all dogs, cats, and ferrets; keeping your cats and ferrets inside and your dogs under direct supervision; calling animal control to remove stray animals from your neighborhood; and having your pets spayed or neutered.

While it is difficult to discern individual species, bats as a group are easy to identify. For this reason we profile one of the most common for Chicago and the United States, the Big Brown bat (see page 37).

DEER

Things That Go Bump in the Night: Animals and Automobiles

We humans are by far the most dangerous mammal to each other and also to virtually all other animals. It's not just that we obliterate acres of wildlife habitat every day, often for asphalt. It's also that we smash critters with our cars as we motor through their lives, crossing their long-established patterns of migration, mating, and food gathering. This is certainly tragedy enough for the animals, but it can pose a genuine, even lethal, danger to you if you hit a good-sized mammal with your car. Even an encounter with a relatively small mammal, such as a raccoon or a possum, can generate problems depending on your defensive driving strategies. The most common and substantially damaging collisions are with deer. According to the National Highway Traffic Safety Administration, there are about 1 million car accidents with deer each year that kill

200 Americans, cause more than 10,000 personal injuries, and result in $1 billion in vehicle damage. By comparison, sharks have killed 10 people in the U.S. in the past 10 years, according to the International Shark Attack File. As for bears, a list of known attacks maintained by Bearplanet.org says about 28 people have been killed by bears in the past decade.

Oh, Deer!

Estimates place the white-tailed deer population in the U.S. at about 1 million around 1900. Today, in part because predators like the cougar and wolf have been removed from the food chain, there are more than 20 million and their number are rising. Differences in the amount of forest cover, agriculture, and human population density, however, have contributed to a patchwork of densities.

Deer have adapted remarkably well, foraging along forest edges and in forests with a significant understory of young trees, shrubs, and plants. Where wildlife managers once faced the problem of too few deer, they now face the problem of too many because deer love habitat comprised of agricultural lands alongside forests, and in many areas fewer people are hunting deer.

Tim Van Deelen, deer research specialist at the Wisconsin Department of Natural Resources and former ecologist with the Illinois Natural History Survey spoke to *Chicago Wilderness Magazine* about the expanding deer population. "You're talking suburban Chicago, a relatively mild climate from the point of view of deer, a virtually unlimited food supply year round, and these deer are putting out fawns at almost the physiological maximum for the species," Van Deelen said.

There are too many deer, indeed, if you have ever tried to dodge one with your car. Diana's story is typical.

> *I was driving home from a lovely dinner at a friend's home on a two-lane road in a fairly developed but still wooded suburban area. It was about midnight, late in the fall. I recall there wasn't much moonlight, but even if the moon had been shining like a streetlight I don't think I could have avoided the deer that bounded out of nowhere at a right angle to my car. Straight across the hood she dove. All I had time to see was the fur of her flank as she bounced across my car. I don't think I even had time to brake.*
>
> *I stopped and saw, to my extreme dismay, she was lying along the other side of the road. I tried to approach her to see how badly she was hurt, but before I could even get close she staggered to her feet, hobbling and dragging herself into the night and beyond my ability to help her. I called the police and the highway patrol*

{ mammals }

and anybody else I could think of to try to find her and get her some help. Later I learned it's common for deer to stagger into the woods and die after they have been hit by a car.

WHITE-TAILED DEER

I remember her clearly, and I still have regret when I think about the accident, but I also recall how there was nothing I could do to prevent it. If she had wanted to "commit deer suicide," she couldn't have picked a better moment to plunge from out of the darkness into my car.

I was very lucky. My car needed work, but the repair shop told me sometimes deer slide right into the windshield and break through, causing death or serious injury for the driver. I always watch the roadsides intently now, looking for that taupe flash of flank or maybe that iridescent shining from any animal's eye. I like to think God knew the animals were going to need reflective eyes one day so we could see them from our cars at night. I'm always watching for that shining, hoping I never hit another animal.

When?

The risk of colliding with deer is greater during the October–January mating season. November has the highest number of collisions. Peak hours for these crashes are from 5 p.m. to 1 a.m. (over half of the total crashes) followed by 5 a.m. to 8 a.m. Vehicle damage from deer collisions averages about $3,100 per claim nationally. Crashes that include bodily injury could increase costs significantly.

Driving Defensively to Dodge Deer

☞ Be alert! Deer are most active at dawn and dusk. Drive slowly and cautiously, scanning the road and roadside, especially at sunrise and sunset when transitional lighting and shadows can play tricks on your vision.

☞ Also know that deer can try to cross busy roads in broad daylight, so always stay on guard.

☞ Even heavily populated suburbs may have deer that have lost more suitable habitat, so don't assume anything.

White-Tailed Deer a.k.a. Virginia Deer
(Odocoileus virginianus)

- Deer pose a threat that can be fatal when they collide with automobiles.
- While often associated with forests, many deer are an ecotonal species that live in transitional areas between forests and thickets (for cover) and prairie and savanna.
- Taking does and bucks into account, white-tails weigh roughly 90–300 pounds. Adult body length is 52–95 inches. The coat is a reddish-brown in the spring and summer and turns to a gray-brown throughout the fall and winter. The deer can be recognized by the characteristic white underside to its tail, which it shows as a signal of alarm by raising the tail during escape.
- White-tailed deer eat large varieties of food, commonly foraging on plants, including shoots, leaves, cacti, and grasses. They also eat acorns, fruit, and corn. Their diet varies by season to include hay, grass, and white clover. White-tailed deer have been known to opportunistically feed on nesting songbirds, field mice, and birds trapped in mist nets.
- Whitetails mate in late October into November, which means they will be on the move during those often rainy times of shortening days. One to three fawns are born in late spring.
- Life expectancy can be up to 15 years, but the average is 2 years for males and 3 years for females in the wild.
- Coyotes attacking fawns are the only natural deer predators of any impact because of the removal of the wolf and cougar from the food chain.
- Deer are able to run up to 40 mph, jump 9-foot fences, and swim 13 mph.
- Antlers do not indicate age as much as they do diet. A better indication of age is the length of the snout and the color of the coat, with older deer tending to have longer snouts and grayer coats

☞ Actively watch for deer where roads pass through wooded and agricultural areas.
☞ Deer crossing signs indicate where heavily used deer trails cross roadways. Slow down and watch for the eye-shine of deer near the road edges. At the very least, obey the speed limit, particularly at night in areas with deer crossing signs.

{ mammals }

☞ Be especially cautious during seasons of high deer activity. October to January is the breeding season (and also includes hunting season when deer are motivated to move), and May to June is when yearlings are seeking new territories.

☞ Deer are often dazed or confused by vehicle headlights. If you see a deer along the roadside, reduce your speed, tap the brakes to alert other vehicles, and try to scare the deer by flashing lights or sounding the horn.

☞ Watch for other deer following the first one that you see. Many times deer travel in groups.

☞ Removing vegetation from roadsides reduces the attraction for deer to feed there. Likewise, do not throw food refuse such as banana peels or apple cores from your car window. Their proximity to the road encourages wildlife of all kinds to search that margin for food.

☞ When you know a collision is unavoidable, experts recommend that you steer straight ahead to minimize losing control and colliding with oncoming traffic or hitting an object off the road.

Roadkill—It's What's for Dinner

Individuals who wish to claim a deer killed in a vehicle collision must report the possession of the road-kill deer to the Illinois Department of Natural Resources. Road-kill deer may only be claimed by those individuals who are:

   ☞ Residents of Illinois.

   ☞ Are not delinquent in child support payments.

   ☞ Do not have their wildlife privileges suspended in any state.

Individuals claiming road-kill deer must report the possession within 24 hours, using the new, easily found online IDNR Road Kill Deer Reporting Form. Possession may also be reported to the IDNR by phoning (217) 782-6431 no later than 4:30 p.m. on the next business day. Individuals involved in deer-vehicle accidents who do not want to take possession of the deer are not required to file a report with the IDNR. It is illegal to take a deer carcass without reporting the incident.

Whistling for Deer

To reduce the number of deer-vehicle collisions, several manufacturers have developed "deer whistles" to mount on the front bumper of an automobile. The theory is that these whistles emit ultrasonic sounds that are frightening to deer, and they claim that their use will significantly reduce the rate of deer-vehicle collisions. Your insurance company may even offer a discount if you install this device on your automobiles.

The usefulness of the deer whistle is in doubt. However, if you've hit a deer, you'll probably do almost anything to avoid a repeat experience. So if installing a whistle makes you more alert to deer, that's a good thing. On the other hand, if it lulls you into a false sense of security, that's a bad thing. Wildlife experts and officials agree that there is no substitute for driver education and awareness of the areas, seasons, and times of day of vulnerability. And many other species merit watching out for when you're driving. It's the least we can do for ourselves and for them.

CONTRACTING DISEASES FROM MAMMALS

Histoplasmosis

Histoplasmosis is a disease caused by the fungus *Histoplasma capsulatum*. Its symptoms vary greatly, but the disease primarily affects the lungs. Occasionally, other organs are affected. This form of the disease is called disseminated histoplasmosis, and it can be fatal if untreated.

Positive skin tests occur in as many as 80 percent of the people living in areas where fungus is common, such as the eastern and central United States, including Illinois. Chicago is within the area that the Center for Disease Control labels as "moderately endemic" for histoplasmosis. Infants, young children, and older persons, in particular those with chronic lung disease, are at increased risk for severe disease. Disseminated disease is more frequently seen in people with cancer, AIDS, or other forms of immunosuppression.

The Critter Connection

Histoplasmosis fungus grows in soil and material contaminated with bat or bird droppings. Accordingly, the fungus has been found in poultry house litter, caves, areas harboring bats, and in bird roosts. So avoid these areas. When contaminated soil is disturbed, the fungal spores take to the air. Breathing the spores causes infection; humans do not transmit the disease.

Symptoms

If symptoms occur, they will start within 3 to 17 days after exposure; the average is 10 days.

Most infected persons have no apparent ill effects. The acute respiratory disease is characterized by:

- A general ill feeling
- Respiratory symptoms
- A dry or nonproductive cough
- Chest pains
- Fever

{ mammals }

Treatment

Doctors use antifungal medications to treat severe cases of acute histoplasmosis and all cases of chronic and disseminated disease. Mild versions of the disease usually resolve without treatment. If you are reinfected, a previous infection usually results in partial protection against ill effects. For a list of doctors in Chicago who treat and diagnose histoplasmosis, go to http://www.lifescript.com/doctor-directory/condition/h-histoplasmosis-il-chicago-h.aspx

Toxoplasmosis

A single-celled parasite called *Toxoplasma gondii* causes a disease known as toxoplasmosis. While the parasite is found throughout the world, more than 60 million people in the United States may be infected with the Toxoplasma parasite. Of those who are infected, very few have symptoms because a healthy person's immune system usually keeps the parasite from causing illness. However, pregnant women and individuals who have compromised immune systems should be cautious. For them a Toxoplasma gondii infection could cause serious health problems.

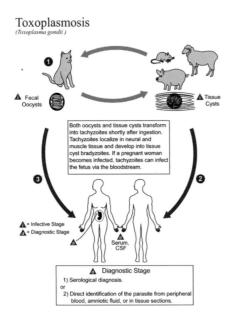

Toxoplasmosis
(Toxoplasma gondii)

Feline Findings

Unfortunately, our beloved cats can play an important role in the spread of toxoplasmosis. They may become infected by eating infected rodents, birds, or other small animals. The parasite is then passed in the cat's feces in oocysts (microscopic parasites).

Kittens and cats can shed millions of these parasites in their feces for as long as three weeks after infection. Mature cats are less likely to shed Toxoplasma if they have been previously infected. A Toxoplasma-infected cat that is shedding the parasite in its feces contaminates the litter box. If the cat is allowed outside, it can contaminate the soil or water in the environment as well.

46

You do not have to get rid of your cat. Cats only spread Toxoplasma in their feces for a few weeks following infection with the parasite. Like humans, cats rarely have symptoms when first infected, so most people do not know if their cat has been infected. The infection will go away on its own; therefore, it does not help to have your cat or your cat's feces tested for Toxoplasma.

People can accidentally swallow the oocyst form of the parasite. This can occur from:

- ☛ Accidental ingestion of oocysts after cleaning a cat's litter box when the cat has shed Toxoplasma in its feces. As mentioned above in "Regarding Cats," scoop the litter boxes of indoor/outdoor cats daily to decrease or even eliminate the risk of "toxo" because the infective life-cycle stage requires at least a day after being shed by the cat to become infectious.
- ☛ Accidental ingestion of oocysts after touching or ingesting anything that has come into contact with a cat's feces that contain Toxoplasma.
- ☛ Accidental ingestion of oocysts in contaminated soil (for example, by not washing hands after gardening or eating unwashed fruits or vegetables from a garden).
- ☛ Drinking water contaminated with the Toxoplasma parasite.

Tularemia

Tularemia, also known as rabbit fever, is a disease that can affect both animals and humans. It is caused by a bacteriun, *Francisella tularensis*. Although mainly wild animals are infected (hares, rabbits, squirrels, muskrats, beavers, deer), occasionally certain domestic animals can be infected (sheep and cats). The rabbit is the species most often involved in disease outbreaks, but the bacteria can also be found in ticks and deer flies.

Tularemia is a sporadic disease that occurs endemically; that is, outbreaks generally are restricted to a particular area or region. Since 1939, there has been a steady decline in the number of cases reported, and currently in the U.S. an average of 120 cases per year are seen. From 2001 through 2010 there were two cases in the Chicago area.

The highest incidents occur in the Midwest during the summer months when ticks are common, and east of the Mississippi during the winter when cottontail rabbits are hunted.

Who Gets Tularemia?

Hunters, trappers, or others who spend a great deal of time outdoors are at a greater risk of exposure to tularemia than people with other occupational or recreational interests.

{ mammals }

How Is Tularemia Spread?

Many routes of human exposure to the tularemia bacteria are known to exist.

The common courses include:

- ☛ Inoculation of the skin or mucous membranes with blood or tissue while handling, dressing, or skinning infected animals.
- ☛ Contact with fluids from infected flies or ticks.
- ☛ The bite of infected ticks.
- ☛ Handling or eating insufficiently cooked rabbit or hare meat that can retain its power of infection even after being frozen for several years.

Less common means of spread are:

- ☛ Drinking contaminated water.
- ☛ Inhaling dust from contaminated soil.
- ☛ Handling contaminated pelts or paws of animals.

Tularemia cannot be spread from one person to another. Patients who recover from tularemia will develop a degree of immunity, but reinfection is possible.

Symptoms of Tularemia

Symptoms develop within 1 to 14 days, usually within 3 to 5 days.

- ☛ Tularemia is usually recognized by the presence of a skin lesion and swollen glands, sometimes at the point of infection. These may be accompanied by the sudden onset of high fever.
- ☛ Ingestion of the organism may produce a throat infection, intestinal pain, diarrhea, and vomiting.
- ☛ Inhalation of the organism may produce a fever alone or combined with a pneumonia-like illness.

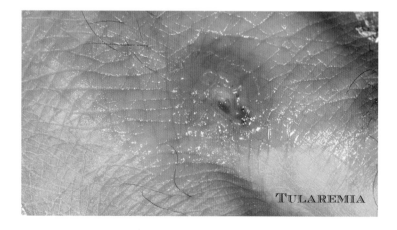

TULAREMIA

Treatment of Tularemia

Tularemia can be difficult to diagnose. It is a rare disease, and the symptoms can be mistaken for other more common illnesses. For this reason, it is important to share with your health care provider any likely exposures, such as tick and deerfly bites, or contact with sick or dead animals. Blood tests and cultures can help confirm the diagnosis. Treatment usually lasts 10 to 21 days depending on the stage of illness and the medication used. Although symptoms may last for several weeks, most patients completely recover.

If you think you have tularemia, contact your physician right away. Upon diagnostic confirmation through laboratory tests, you can take antibiotics for the disease. Long-term immunity follows recovery, but reinfection has been reported. Without therapy, fatality rates are 5 percent (ulceroglandular) to 30 percent (pneumonic). The mortality rate is about 6 percent or about seven people per year nationally.

Preventing Tularemia

- ☞ Wear rubber gloves when skinning or handling animals, especially rabbits.
- ☞ Cook wild game, especially rabbit and squirrel meat, thoroughly before eating.
- ☞ Avoid bites of flies and ticks by the use of protective clothing and insect repellents, and check for ticks frequently.
- ☞ Avoid drinking untreated water.
- ☞ Instruct children not to handle any sick or dead animals.

RACCOON

COYOTE PUP

BABY
OPOSSUM

ROTTWEILER

insects &
arachnids

This is the deadliest chapter. If you are going to have a fatal or life-threatening encounter with another creature, other than another human, it will likely be with an insect or an arachnid, or the disease organisms they carry. (Remember, though, this is highly, highly unlikely.) Some of this probability derives from the sheer number of these creatures. In the United States there are approximately 91,000 described species of insects, plus at least 71,000 undescribed species. What does this mean in terms of insect proximity? "A whole lotta crawlin,' creepin,' and flyin' goin' on." Soil samples in North Carolina 5 inches deep yielded an estimated 124 million animals per acre. Similar studies in Pennsylvania produced an estimated 425 million animals per acre. If you walk through a grassy field you will likely be sharing the great outdoors with literally thousands of arachnids, mostly spiders, which, we hasten to add, almost definitely will not harm you.

Before the idea of these creepy crawlies overwhelms you, keep in mind several things. The vast majority of these creatures are not only beneficial to life on earth—they are absolutely essential to it. Imagine a planet without "sanitary engineer" insects to break down the bodies of all the dead or to process fecal matter back into the food chain. A world without the pollination of fruits, vegetables, nuts, and flowers would be a barren wasteland indeed. As the bee said to the plant, "Honey, you need me. Without me you'd lose your bloomers." And without spiders and other predatory insects, you would have to rely more on pesticides to keep the insects in their place, hardly a healthy solution in the long run.

The primary thing to remember is that only a tiny handful of these insects and arachnids are dangerous to humans. The great bulk of major episodes involve cases of anaphylactic shock—an allergic reaction to a sting that is immediately treatable *if* you know you are at risk, and some 1 to 2 million Americans are. True, some very dangerous illnesses are carried by insects, and we will examine these. You should not disregard spider and tick bites either.

What Are Insects and Arachnids?

Creatures from the Insecta and Arachnida classes are all arthropods, meaning they belong to the phylum of creatures that have jointed legs and a hard exoskeleton that protects their organs and gives their bodies shape. Despite their myriad appearances, adult insects have three pairs of jointed legs and three body parts (head, thorax, and abdomen). On insect heads you'll find their eyes (often of the compound type), a pair of antennae, and mouthparts. The thorax has three segments, each with its own pair of legs. Wings, if present, will be found on segments two or three. The abdomen, which does not usually have appendages, has a hind tip called the terminalia. This is where the insect has its egg-laying, mating, or defensive equipment. The stingers of wasps and bees,

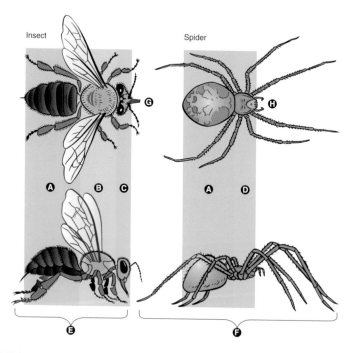

Both insects and arachnids have an abdomen (A). Insects have two more segments: the thorax (B) and head (C), whereas in arachnids the two are fused into the cephalothorax (D). The most visible difference is that insects have six legs (E) while arachnids have eight legs (F). Lastly, insects have two antennae and two compound eyes (G), while arachnids have two chelicerae and eight simple eyes (H).

for example, are found here. Other insect groups include mosquitoes, blackflies, biting midges, and lice.

Arachnids, on the other hand, have four pairs of legs, no antennae, and only two body sections because (with a few exceptions) their head and thorax are joined into one form called the cephalothorax. Arachnids include spiders, scorpions, ticks, and mites.

To the average person, if a creature crawls on more than four legs, it's an insect. But as we mentioned earlier, insects are just one of the major types of arthropods; arachnids are the other. Arachnids include spiders, ticks, mites, and scorpions (not a concern in Illinois), but often when people speak of arachnids, they are generally referring to spiders, including tarantulas (not a concern in Illinois). Spiders are the largest group of arachnids, so it is fitting that the Greek word for spider, "arachne," gives the gang its name. Arachne was a young girl who bested the goddess Athena in a weaving contest. After Athena tore the winning work into pieces, Arachne hanged herself in despair. Athena loosed the rope and saved her life, but the rope was changed into a cobweb and Arachne became a spider.

Like snakes, spiders sometimes generate fear (in this case, arachnophobia) in people, a fear that is quite real, but is, as you will see, disproportionate to the dangers involved. If you shudder at spiders, though, you are not alone. Remember, for the little miss in the Mother Goose rhyme, "all it took was just one look."

> *Little Miss Muffet, sat on a tuffet,*
> *Eating her curds and whey;*
> *Along came a spider, who sat down beside her*
> *And frightened Miss Muffet away.*

BEES AND WASPS

In the scientific world, these creatures are grouped in the order Hymenoptera. The name refers to their "membrane wings" because all of these insects have two pairs of clear, window-like wings, and the females have an abdomen that ends in an egg-laying organ and/or a stinger. Ants are also in this group because at a certain stage of life they do have wings, at which point they are often mistaken for termites. Many ants have stingers, too, and we'll talk about the most potent species in depth later in this chapter. Some of these creatures can give you a serious problem, but generally only if you are prone to anaphylactic shock (see more below on this medical emergency condition) or if you provoke multiple stings. If that happens, then pardon me, but they have the wings, and you need the prayer.

{ insects & arachnids }

Oh So Social and Solitary

There is another useful way to think about Hymenoptera: Are they social or solitary spirits? This point fascinates scientists because the Hymenoptera fill the spectrum. Honeybees, famous for their organized social structure, are at one extreme. At this end of the scale you'll also find the bumblebees and the true wasps, which include hornets and yellow jackets in their family. These insects are considered to be "eusocial," meaning truly social.

Eusocial insects exhibit both cooperation in division of labor and reproduction expressed within overlapping generations. For example, in honeybees there is a sharp division between the sterile caste of female soldiers and workers and the reproductive caste comprised of the queen and her male drones. In executing her duties, a soldier will defend the nest by spraying, stinging, or biting intruders, and a worker will enhance the nest, care for the eggs, larvae, pupae, and queen, and forage for food. Male drones live only long enough to fertilize the potential millions of eggs laid by the queen. This famous social structure has an extra dimension to it: the ultimate self-sacrifice of life the soldiers make to defend the nest or colony so that the gene pool survives. Some people have called this cooperative behavior "biological altruism." What this means is that eusocial insects have absolutely no qualms about attacking you in defense of their nest, even if it means certain death for them. They also have powerful venom to achieve their purposes.

But not all Hymenoptera are eusocial. At the other end of the spectrum are the solitary species such as carpenter bees (the big ones that bore holes in your garage roof supports); sweat bees (the small ones that sting you mildly when you are working to repair the garage roof); and the mud or dirt daubers of the digger wasp family (the mysterious ones you wonder about that have built those mud tubes on your garage walls). It's a little confusing, I know. It would be simpler if all "bees" and "wasps" were eusocial and that was that, but nature just won't cooperate that way. Think of it as a big family where some of the brothers and sisters are nurses and some are writers. Their daily lives and contributions are quite different, but the individuals are closely related and may even resemble each other physically.

The reason all of this matters is that in contrast to the eusocial insects that have the powerful stinging venom, the sting of the solitary bees and wasps is usually a much less powerful and usually less painful sting. Scientists disagree on this distinction, however, perhaps because pain is a relative experience. To avoid all pain, avoid studiously all the species described in this section.

I'll describe the individual eusocial and solitary Hymenoptera you're likely to encounter in the creature profiles later in this chapter, but mainly when I talk about "bees" (including hornets and yellow jackets) here, I'll be generally addressing the powerful eusocial species whose stings you especially want to avoid. I'll specify when talking exclusively about honeybees or bumblebees or yellow jackets, for example, but when I just say "bee" or "bees," I'm referring to eusocial insects in general.

How Bees Sting

Soldier bees, all female, will sting you in defense of the nest with their modified ovipositors (egg-laying apparatus) located on the end of the abdomen. In honeybees, that sting is barbed in such a way that once it penetrates, say, the skin of a human, it cannot be extracted. The honeybee soldier must pull away, leaving her sting and venom sac in you (along with some of her internal organs). With much of her abdomen then ripped away, she is destined to die. Meanwhile, her stinger continues to inject venom into you, the presumed attacker, even after the soldier has retreated. No matter whether the bee has left her stinger in you or not, something even more powerful has happened. She has also sent a chemical telegram to her cohorts that says, "Come and sting the daylights out of this aggressor right now, and here's a map of how to reach him!"

HONEYBEE

A honeybee stinger is barbed, and it cannot be extracted once used (1). After a soldier bee has retreated, the stinger, venom sac, and some of the bee's internal organs remain behind (2). The stinger continues pumping venom and sending out a chemical alarm to other bees; the bee that left its stinger eventually dies.

How Some Bees Communicate:
Dancing, Smelling, and Belly-Rubbing

Communication among the eusocial insects involves a complex and powerful network of behaviors and adaptations differently applied to various situations. To give you an example of the forces at work, let's look at food-gathering communication. Once again, the honeybees have elevated this exceptional and mysterious connective ability literally to an art form: they dance. The round or circle dance indicates nectar and pollen supplies within 80 feet. Other honeybees read the dance by sensing air vibrations and touching the dancer's antennae. In the even more remarkable waggle dance, the dancer indicates food sources more than 320 feet away from the nest by dancing a figure-eight shape that indicates distance and direction relative to the position of the sun. In the vibration dance, a worker vibrates its belly while in contact with other honeybees. In this way honeybees are rallied to the waggle dance to increase food foraging.

Other bees have their own means of transmitting messages. For example, a second and extremely powerful communication channel for bees is the distribution of pheromones, species-specific chemicals released to stimulate a specific behavioral or physiological response. These pheromones are invisible and linger in the air long enough to

WHAT TO DO IF A BEE STINGS YOU

If you only have one or just a few insects on you, try to remain calm and brush them from your skin promptly with deliberate movements to prevent additional stings. Then, quietly and immediately leave the area.

Next, look for a stinger that resembles a small wood splinter still embedded at the point of attack. If you see one, you have been stung once by a honeybee.

- Remove the stinger by scraping it away with a fingernail, a knife, a credit card, or something similar. If you do this within 30 seconds, you will reduce the impact of the sting. Even a few seconds either way can make a big difference. Contrary to conventional advice, grasping the stinger does not increase the venom dose.
- Proceed as below.

Other bees and wasps do not leave their stingers. If no stinger is present, do the following:

- Wash the wound with soap and water and apply an antiseptic.
- Apply a cold compress. Ice should help reduce the swelling, though it should not be applied directly to skin.
- Elevate the affected arm or leg and apply ice or a cold compress to reduce swelling and pain.
- Pain may be reduced by the application of a paste (poultice) of meat tenderizer and water.
- Use topical steroid ointments or oral antihistamines to relieve itching.
- For stings in the mouth or throat, suck on ice and seek medical attention right away.
- If blisters form, gently clean them with soap and water to prevent secondary infections; do not break blisters.
- See your doctor if swelling progresses or if the sting site seems infected.

get the job done. So, for example, when a bee is injured she releases pheromones to summon the troops to pick up the fight. Because of the tightly woven social structure within the hive, you can be sure that more soldiers will respond to her call, even if it means their deaths, too, in defense of the nest.

Hive Jive: When Are They Jumpin'?

In their near-perfect progression toward survival, bees have predictable cycles of activity based on the time of year. Typically, the queen spends the winter in the hive with a small staff of workers, and they begin expanding the existing colony or building a new one in the spring. In spring, swarms may be observed as the colony searches for a new location to live as new queens and young workers take flight from old crowded hives

{ insects & arachnids }

with younger workers in search of the right spot. As the queen tires, the swarm lands on something, such as a tree branch, where the colony can stay huddled together, protecting her while a few scout bees continue the search. Because a swarm is in essence a group of homeless bees, they are less protective than they might be about the hive, so they are not as likely to sting because they do not feel as defensive. Remember, though, that protection of the queen is always an issue. As for making the bees leave, it is best to let them stay put. They will probably move on to a more out-of-the-way place to secure a nest in a day or two.

Once the new location is selected, nest building and egg laying begins. The queen's body may hold millions of eggs, and she will likely lay most of these in her lifetime. These eggs will be fertilized by the male drones while the female workers and soldiers attend to nest building, caring for the hive and its young, and food production. Drones are most numerous during the summer, but as food becomes scarce toward the fall, the workers kill them by stinging and remove them from the hive. Fall is another season when swarming may occur because the hive becomes too large. Winter activity in the hive depends on the food supply. On warmer winter days, workers may leave the hive in search of early blooming flowers.

The bottom line on the bee calendar is this: Do not assume that you cannot be stung in the winter. It is true that your risk is diminished compared to summer's frequent activity, but you can be stung at any time of year.

Experienced beekeepers have also noted that bees are in better moods on bright, sunny days. Like us, they seem to be more moody and irritable on rainy, cooler days.

Bees settle down into the hive at night after a hard day's work, but they can certainly be disturbed after dark, so if you know of a nest, treat it with respect at all times.

"Where the Bees Are . . ."

Our bee friends can be found in many types of habitats: beneath stones and wood; in the ground; near water; in living wood and rotting wood; and, of course, near flowering plants and at picnics, especially if soft drinks, sweets, or beer are on the menu. Picture a bear gouging for

HOW DO BEES FLY?

Honeybees "make a beeline"—that is, a straight or direct course. However, other eusocial and solitary bees and wasps tend to exhibit loopy flight patterns.

honey with its paw stuck in an old log or in the hollow of a tree—that's what you *don't* want to do. Nor do you want to walk barefoot in blooming clover, as appealing as that sounds.

A rule of thumb is that the activity of the hive is a private affair, so be prepared to be surprised.

These insects require and are adept at seeking shelter, so they may want to "freeload" on you, setting up residence in your garage, for example. Wasp and hornet nests suspended from house eaves and from tree branches are obvious places to avoid. (In general, the term "hornet" is used for species that nest above ground, and the term "yellow jacket" for those that make subterranean nests.) All species are social, living in colonies of hundreds to thousands of individuals.

Should you locate one around your house, call the Cook County agricultural extension agent at (773) 768-7779 for advice on how to remove it. Several sprays are commercially available to kill the insects, but should you decide to eliminate them yourself, use extreme caution. Many people have suffered multiple stings by incurring the anger of the whole hive. Likewise, children anger them by throwing rocks at hives.

Why Bees Sting You

Bees and their close kin—we'll talk about ants shortly—are not aggressive by nature. While this may be hard to believe if you've been stung, try to remember what you were doing that triggered the insects' defensive response.

For example, Geneva tells this story:

It was midday, probably in late July or August. It was really hot outside, but rain was coming in and I wanted to get the grass cut that day. I cranked up the mower. It was not exactly a whisper-jet model, but none of them are. I'd been mowing my yard for about an hour, so I was pretty sweaty. All of a sudden, yellow jackets were flying all around me and stinging me like fire! Where had they come from? I had no idea! I started trying to swat them off me, and just by instinct I ran from where I was being stung. I think I even took off my clothes right there in the neighborhood to get them off me!

What happened? Geneva had unwittingly called out the cavalry. To the yellow jackets, whose nest was underground, the lawnmower sounded like the equivalent of a "chopper" squadron suddenly appearing right over your house—ready to open fire, for all you know. In short, it angered the insects mightily. Their pheromone alarm was set off, and, of course,

{ insects & arachnids }

Geneva's sweat didn't calm the defenders down, nor did the fact that she started swatting at them. (Not swatting while being stung takes a supreme amount of will, I might add.) The time of day and year played a part, too. Already very active, the yellow jackets were certain to respond at midday. Because it was later in the summer, the yellow jackets were naturally more aggressive.

In another case, again in late summer, a car pulled into a gravel driveway next to a yellow jacket nest only 5 feet away on the ground. A young Bible salesman got out of the car and stepped very close to the nest, not knowing it was there. Whether it was the engine sound, his footfall, or a combination of these factors, the yellow jackets set out after him. He started running and was picked up down the street, but he suffered multiple stings before he could escape.

HOW MUCH DOES A STING HURT?

The list below indicates relative pain measures (0-low to 4-high) for some species discussed in this chapter. A range of numbers represents a variation in sting pain levels.

Spider wasp 4	Hornet 2	Velvet ant 1–2
Harvester ant 3	Bumblebee 2	Sweat bee* 0–1
Paper wasp 0–3		

* The sweat bee was not part of this survey, but is included here because it is frequently encountered.

0   No pain. The result of encounters with insects whose stingers are too small or weak to penetrate human skin.

1   Pain so slight as to constitute no real deterrent. Sting is perceived, but most people do not say it "hurts."

2   Painful. The great mass of painful stings.

3   Sharply and seriously painful. Differentiated from level 2 pain by the production of, apart from any surprise or fear, loud cries, groans, and/or long preoccupation with the pain.

4   Traumatically painful. Often medically serious events with strong physical reactions and long-lasting pain.

The relative pain scale above was adapted from "A Pain Scale for Bee, Wasp, and Ant Stings," a scientific paper by Christopher K. Starr, ("A Simple Pain Scale for Field Comparison of Hymenopteran Stings," *Journal of Entomological Science,* vol. 20, no. 2:225–31, published by the Georgia Entomological Society.)

In both cases, while the insects seemed like the aggressors, in fact they were only protecting the thing they care most about in life: their extended and extensive family.

More Stinging Stories

Yellow jackets are especially menacing because they often build their paper nests underground, and it's common to invoke their wrath without any foreknowledge. Hornets, on the other hand, are wasps that build their nests, also of paper, above ground where you can generally see them. Nevertheless, the story below indicates how easy it is to get into trouble with them, and one way you might get out of it. The story is set in Tennessee, but Chicago paddlers can benefit from it.

Juanita has been an outdoorswoman her whole life. She grew up in the panhandle of Florida in the 1940s and 50s when it teemed with wildlife, before it was crowded by the people who are now discovering its wondrous beauty. Her daddy took her on his fishing expeditions where he would gently prod the snakes resting in the trees with his boat paddle "just to see which way they'd fall—in the boat or out of it." Juanita dryly adds, "I developed a strong prayer life early on." When Juanita was teaching paddling she cautioned people that there are two primary dangers on the river: the white-water rapids and the hornet nests in the overhanging tree branches. She tells this story:

> "I had a young woman in the front of my canoe who was just learning to paddle. We had eddied out on the Hiwassee River for a breather, and even though I had given this group of students my standard warnings, she reached up to grip a tree branch without looking to see that it housed a hornet's nest. I saw what was about to happen, but before I could stop her she had inadvertently rattled their nest by grasping the branch. Out they came! Right on time and mad as you-know-what. I yelled to her, "Dive in the water and swim away now! I'll pick you up in the canoe. Do it!" The novice took the advice and plunged in the river. Staying above water in the canoe, Juanita sustained a few stings, but she saved the girl from that pain because the hornets can't dive into the water to sting.

One lesson of this story is that if you can submerge yourself safely in water and swim away from the scene of the attack, by all means do so. When you come up for air, do so briefly and resubmerge as soon as possible so the hornets won't be able to sting your face and neck. Try to swim at least 5 yards away if you can, more if possible, to slip away from their defensive anger.

{ insects & arachnids }

63

Who's Got the Worst Temper?

The cliché "mad as a hornet" might make you think that hornets top the list, but not all hornets are equally defensive. Yellow jackets are probably tied with them for first place. Other paper wasps are probably somewhat more tolerant of the kinds of minor disturbances created by people than are hornets or yellow jackets. When it comes to bees, it depends on the strain. So really, it makes the best sense to treat all these insects with equal respect.

Anaphylactic Shock: A Life and Death Situation

The majority of insect bite or sting cases that result in fatal or major medical episodes are cases involving anaphylactic shock. This is a form of allergic reaction.

Allergic reactions to stings range from mild to severe. When the reaction is massive and immediate it is called "anaphylaxis," which is a life-threatening situation. These reactions result from the body's release of antibodies to combat the sting venom. Severe allergic reactions occur when the body overproduces these antibodies, and some medical authorities hold that subsequent stings tend to produce increasingly more severe allergic reactions in those already sensitized. For this reason anaphylactic shock is more common in adults than in children, who have generally not had the opportunity to be stung as much as adults. Despite this tendency, reactions to subsequent stings are still largely unpredictable.

BALDFACED
HORNET

Untreated anaphylaxis can prove fatal in 5 to 30 minutes. About 60 to 80 percent of the time, death results from an inability to breathe due to swollen airways that prevent airflow to the lungs. Other deaths are triggered when blood vessels dilate or expand so much that blood flow to vital organs is reduced to fatal levels.

Severity of the sting can depend on the location. Wounds on the neck can affect breathing, and swallowing a yellow jacket (who craves the sugar in your soft drinks) can result in a sting inside your throat that can cause strangulation. (For a close call of this type of episode, see "Sweet Sugar" below.)

According to the National Jewish Medical and Research Center's "Lung Line," if you are at the extreme end of the insect venom sensitivity scale, any insect bite can trigger an allergic reaction that may result in anaphylactic shock. This includes the less powerful sting of solitary insects such as sweat bees.

Symptoms of Anaphylactic Shock

After an insect sting, watch for these conditions:
- ☞ Soreness and swelling not only at the sight of the sting, but also on other parts of the body.
- ☞ Fever and/or chills.
- ☞ Joint or muscle pain.
- ☞ Sneezing, coughing, or wheezing.
- ☞ Shortness of breath.
- ☞ Tightness and swelling in the throat.
- ☞ Tightness in the chest.
- ☞ Severe itching, burning, rash, or hives on the skin beyond the sting area.
- ☞ Swelling of face, tongue, mouth, or lymph glands.
- ☞ Blue skin color around lips, mouth, and fingernails.
- ☞ Dizziness or light-headedness.
- ☞ Stomach cramps, nausea, and vomiting.
- ☞ Unconsciousness.

Anaphylactic shock is a severe medical emergency and must be treated immediately with epinephrine, a form of adrenaline. This drug works by opening up airways, causing blood vessels to constrict, and forcing the heart to beat with more vigor.

You can get a "bee sting kit" with antihistamine tablets, alcohol swabs, and a loaded syringe with epinephrine by prescription from your doctor—*before* the medical emergency arises. Do not expect to drive to the drugstore and purchase one at the point of need.

{ insects & arachnids }

Learn how to self-administer the epinephrine according to your doctor's instructions, and replace the device before the clearly labeled expiration date. The shelf life of a kit is about a year, but the fine print in the kit will tell you that if the epinephrine has turned an amber color, it's time to replace it.

Remember that injected epinephrine is rescue medication only, and you must still have someone take you to an emergency room immediately if you are stung. Additional medical treatment may be necessary. Those with severe allergies may want to consider wearing a special bracelet or necklace that identifies the wearer as having severe allergies to insect stings and bites and that supplies other important medical information.

The Buzz Is: Take the Bee Sting Kit with You!

You are at risk for anaphylactic shock if you have increasingly more pronounced reaction to insect stings over time. If this is the case, get an insect sting kit and always have it available. This especially applies if you regularly walk, hike, horseback ride, bike, or camp where epinephrine is more than five minutes away—which means just about everywhere except the hospital. Insect sting kits come with a belt clip to make them easier to take with you.

The recommended storage temperature for epinephrine is 59 to 86 degrees Fahrenheit, so keeping an insect sting kit in the glove compartment of your car is not a good solution, especially in the summer when your risk of stings is highest. If you have one handy, it may prove worth the hassle one day, so put one in your pack, or on your saddle or bike, if not on your belt.

YELLOW JACKET

Long-Term Prevention for Anaphylactic Shock

If you have a severe allergy to insect venom and are concerned because you spend a great deal of time outdoors, consider receiving insect venom immunotherapy, a highly effective vaccination program that actually prevents future allergic sting reactions in 97 percent of treated patients. During immunotherapy, the allergist administers gradually stronger doses of venom extract every few weeks over a period of three to five years. This helps the patient's immune system become more and more resistant to future insect stings. Your allergist can provide you with the proper tests and screening for this type of treatment.

To "Bee" Stung or Not to "Bee" Stung

There are several things you can do to reduce your risk of being stung by all types of bees and wasps:

- ☞ Do wear white or light-colored clothing with a smooth finish. Hunters, for example, should opt for lighter-colored camouflage.
- ☞ Do wear closed-toe shoes outdoors and avoid going barefoot.
- ☞ Do avoid loose-fitting garments that can trap insects between material and skin.
- ☞ Do check your property regularly for bee and wasp colonies. Honeybees, for example, nest in a wide variety of places. Check animal burrows, water meter boxes, loose building siding, overturned flowerpots, trees, and shrubs.
- ☞ Do keep pets and children indoors when using weed trimmers, hedge clippers, tractor power mowers, and chain saws. Attacks frequently occur when a person is mowing the lawn or pruning shrubs and inadvertently strikes a nest above ground (bees, wasps, and hornets) or below ground (yellow jackets).
- ☞ Do avoid excessive motion when near a colony. Bees are much more likely to respond to an object in motion than a stationary one.
- ☞ Do not wear leather, which is reportedly particularly irritating to bees, wasps, hornets, and yellow jackets.
- ☞ Do not wear brightly colored, dark, rough, or wooly material.
- ☞ Do not wear perfumes, lotions (including sunscreen), hair sprays, and other odorous substances.
- ☞ Do not pen, tie, or tether animals near beehives or nests.
- ☞ Do not leave sweet foods or beverages (including diet or sugar-free drinks) in exposed areas as the sugary content will attract stinging insects. (See the "Sweet Sugar" story below.) Avoid garbage collection areas for this same reason.

{ insects & arachnids }

67

"Sweet Sugar"

When you think about it, it's obvious that eusocial and solitary bees and wasps have a sweet tooth—they're nectar-bound. Here's an account from the website of insecticide manufacturer RESCUE! (traps.com/horrorstories.html). Their "Yellow Jacket Horror Stories" contest will make you think twice as you slurp your own sugary concoction in the summer.

> I was recently stung [by a yellow jacket in August] in the back of the mouth after picking up my soda can. I will never forget this experience and hope no one else ever has to go through it either. I was very worried about hearing cases of allergic reactions and what could happen to me. I tried to immediately spit the unknown substance out, but it was too late. The bugger had already stung me. Immediately, there was a rush of stinging in my mouth. I tried to use cold water to dilute the poisonous potion, but it was too late. I was surprised that there was nothing I could do. I thought to myself, "Boy, what a stupid thing to do, leave a can of Coke and then come back 15 minutes later to get stung."
>
> A few years earlier, my boy Robby had been stung by a bee on the lower lip, and it swelled up quickly. We had to rush him to Doctors on Duty because he had an allergic reaction. I thought that this could have been my turn, but I was lucky. The back of my throat became sore immediately. It became very hard to swallow, like a sore throat can be when you have a bad cold.
>
> I tried cold ice water on the back of my throat, tipping my head back, but it only felt good when I left it there, and the pain came back when I swallowed the water. I tried to take Advil, 4 tablets, 1,000 mgs., and started to feel a little better, but still was very uncomfortable when I swallowed. A couple of hours later, still no relief. I thought at this time I was through the allergic stage, and only had to put up with the pain when I swallowed. It was about 9:30 p.m., so I decided to go to bed early. The pain was still present, and I was restless and couldn't fall off to sleep, because I was worried that I would swell up more and lose my breathing. I arose from the bed an hour later and found some Benadryl Elixir, and immediately took 3 teaspoons full and then sat up a few minutes with my family. I went back to bed around 11 p.m., but I still was feeling the wrath of the yellow jacket sting. I finally fell off to sleep 30 minutes later, but tossed and turned all night, waking up every hour or so.
>
> The next morning, about 5 a.m., I still was swollen, and could not swallow without pain. I was surprised that the pain did not go away overnight. I took 3 more Advils and grabbed a cup of coffee

and headed out to work. I was thinking about staying home, but I knew I had to go to work and follow up on a hot job. I tried to eat a piece of fruit, a pear, and my throat felt good when the cool fruit touched it. By noon, the swelling had subsided, and I was getting back to normal. I will never forget this ordeal and hope no one experiences what I went through.

I would like to recommend to everyone out there who knows that there are yellow jackets hovering around, please do not allow yourself or your friends to drink soda pop out of a can!!!!!

Have them put it in a glass or keep their thumb over the can's opening when they are not drinking. Please be aware of what I went through and protect yourself as well as your loved ones.

Don't Sweat It

Bees also get agitated by perspiration odor. This seems to support the thinking of long-time expert beekeeper, L.L. Lanier of Wewahitchka, Florida, who says that bees can tell when you are afraid because you emit an odor of fear that they can detect. It signals to them that an aggressive confrontation is about to begin, so they sting you in advance of the expected attack. While I have not found scientific reporting *per se* to support this theory, it certainly agrees with what we know about pheromones and insects: they use invisible chemical signals to communicate for food gathering, mating, and defense.

A note about sweat bees: Although there are 502 species of Halicitidae in the United States, only about 12 of these are attracted to human sweat. These sweat bees will sting if they are pressed by clothing or trapped in the bend of an arm or a leg, but their sting is not usually very painful and triggers only minor reactions in normally sensitive individuals. However, in extremely sensitive individuals, the sweat bee sting can trigger anaphylactic shock. Sweat bees are most active in Illinois from April through October.

Don't Swat It

Bottom line: Keep your cool around bees, wasps, yellow jackets, and the like. They can detect motion much faster than we can and will most likely read it as an aggressive gesture. When they are simply "buzzing" around you (not stinging), resist the temptation to swat at them. The best defense is to remain motionless or walk away slowly. If just one or a few start to sting you, protect your face with your hands while you walk away, because these insects prefer to sting you here if they can. If necessary and possible, lie still with your face down on the ground.

{ insects & arachnids }

Lunch on the Deck on a Late-Summer Day

It's September and you know that cold weather will come before too long. The desire to have lunch on the (unscreened) deck is irresistible. You make a sandwich and head out with a cold drink. In about 60 seconds, the bees or wasps have arrived to share in your midday repast. This is the perfect situation to exercise your good judgment. You can:

- ☞ Ignore them, which means no swatting, sweating, cursing, or panic. You should, of course, take care not to accidentally ingest one of those flying friends.
- ☞ Just give it up and go back inside. This is the option to take if you or your guests cannot resist swatting at them.
- ☞ Get the insecticide spray and go to work. This is not really a good option because you are outside in their world offering the natural attraction of food. In most cases, even if you kill some hymenopterans with spray, others will be right along behind them.

Danger in Numbers: Make a Run for It!

Humans have used swarms of bees positively and negatively throughout history. As far back as Exodus, which talks about sending hornets to drive out Hivites, Canaanites, and Hittites, people have used bees' proclivity to sting humans and animals ferociously, painfully, and when anatomically possible, repeatedly. Hives were often kept behind the fortified wall of medieval cities and hurled from walls onto the invading enemy, a technique that helped King Henry I of France rout the Duke of Lorraine when his panicked, stung horses led an ignominious and rapid retreat.

If you happen to engage the wrath of a swarm of bees, yellow jackets, or hornets, run as far and fast as you can away from the hive, nest, or whatever the insects were protecting. Do not flail or swing your arms, as this may further annoy them. You can expect to be chased, but not far. Estimates range from 25 to 100 yards for most species. Just keep running, and get to shelter or the closest house or car as quickly as possible. Don't worry if a few bees become trapped in your home. If several bees follow you into your car, drive about a quarter of a mile, lower the windows, and let the bees out of the car.

PAPER WASP

If for some reason you cannot run, you can follow Juanita's course of action. One fall day she was out with a friend who was using a metal detector to search for lost treasures in an old mountain town. Juanita said:

You get in the wrong place at the wrong time. I must have disturbed a yellow jacket nest somehow, because they were swarming all around us—me mostly, so it wasn't the metal detector or anything like that. I had on a long sleeved shirt, fortunately. I was trying to shrink my body inside that shirt with only indifferent success. As the yellow jackets started to sting my hands, I started to talk to myself out loud, 'Just be quiet. Resist the urge to start screaming and running.' I started walking deliberately away and when I reached a distance of about 20 to 30 feet away they had stopped stinging me. Maybe it was or wasn't the right thing to do, but my childhood training had ingrained in me the need not to run in a situation like that. I ended up with about 15 stings on one hand and about 20 on the other. I didn't swell too badly, though, because I was able to play the piano in church that night.

If you aren't physically able to run in a multiple-sting situation, immediately start walking away from the site of attack. Eventually you will reach safety.

Multiple Stings

Juanita was extremely lucky because she was not sensitive to insect venom. According to poison control center experts, multiple stings—30 to 40—will likely cause a severe reaction even in an unsensitized individual, not to mention go a long way toward making the person extremely sensitive to stings in the future. Body weight plays a factor here, too. so The reactions of a slender child to multiple stings will be more extreme than those of a relatively sting-free adult.

Symptoms from such multiple stings can include:

- ☞ Chills
- ☞ Vomiting
- ☞ Breathing difficulty
- ☞ Pulmonary edema (swelling)
- ☞ Fever
- ☞ Collapse
- ☞ Drop in blood pressure

Multiple stings, especially ones that trigger these symptoms, should be attended to by a medical professional or medical emergency response team as soon as possible.

{ insects & arachnids }

(continued on page 76)

Baldfaced Hornet
(Vespula maculata)

BALDFACED HORNET

- This hornet's sting is potentially lethal for those highly allergic and prone to anaphylactic shock. Other reactions vary according to number of stings, location of stings, ratio of venom to body weight, and individual sensitivity.
- The baldfaced hornet is found throughout the continental United States.
- It ranges in size from 0.5 to 0.75 inch.
- Its body is black and white patterned.
- Baldfaced hornets nest in woodlands edges, suburban yards, and meadows.
- These hornets are very commonly found on flowers. In spring, the female chews wood to craft a small, pendant nest of gray pulp; nests can eventually grow to the size of a basketball. The nest is usually suspended high in trees, but may also be near the ground and is always in the open. The doorway to the nest is at the bottom. Adults are extremely protective of the nest and will sting repeatedly in defense of it.

Black-and-Yellow Mud Dauber
(Sceliphron caementarium)

- The mud/dirt dauber's sting is potentially lethal for those highly allergic and prone to anaphylactic shock. Other reactions vary according to number of stings, location of stings, ratio of venom to body weight, and individual sensitivity.
- The mud dauber is common throughout the United States.
- They grow to 1 to 1.25 inches.
- The body is nonmetallic black with yellow markings.

- Nests of parallel earthen tubes are found in a variety of sheltered areas such as meadows under rocks, cliffs under rock overhangs, and in human habitation areas such as under overhanging roofs, outbuildings, sheds, and on the sides of old cars.

BLACK-AND-YELLOW
MUD DAUBER

- Mud daubers can sting painfully. Females can be found at edges of ponds or pools collecting mud to be shaped by their mandibles into balls to form linked tubular cells. Inside these cells the female stuffs a paralyzed spider and an egg that will hatch into a larvae. After feeding on the spider, the young mud dauber will then dig its way out of the closed tube.

Bumblebee (Pyrobombus bimaculatus)

- The bumblee's sting is potentially lethal for those highly allergic and prone to anaphylactic shock. Other reactions vary according to number of stings, location of stings, ratio of venom to body weight, and individual sensitivity.

BUMBLEBEE

- Bumblebees are very common throughout the eastern United States.
- They range in size from 0.4 to 0.8 inch.
- Their hairy bodies are bright yellow and black.
- They nest in ready-made hollows such as deserted mouse nests.
- Bumblebees are extremely important in pollination. Red clover is a prime example, depending on bumblebees for its propagation.

{ insects & arachnids }

73

WILD CHICAGO

Honeybee (Apis mellifera)

- The honeybee's sting is potentially lethal for those highly allergic and prone to anaphylactic shock. Other reactions vary according to number of stings, location of stings, ratio of venom to body weight, and individual sensitivity.

HONEYBEE

- Honeybees are common throughout the United States.
- They range in size from 0.5 to 0.75 inch.
- Honeybees are mostly reddish brown and black with paler rings on the abdomen that are usually yellow-orange. Their wings are translucent, and their heads, legs, and antennae are nearly black.
- Hives are found in hollow trees and in beekeepers' freestanding wooden apiaries. Workers seek flower nectar in meadows, woods, and gardens.
- Imported to North America in the 1600s by European settlers, honeybees are used to pollinate crops as well as produce honey.

Paper Wasp (Polistes spp.)

- Paper wasps' stings are potentially lethal for those highly allergic and prone to anaphylactic shock. Other reactions vary according to number of stings, location of stings, ratio of venom to body weight, and individual sensitivity.
- They are common throughout the United States.
- They grow to 0.5 to 1 inch.
- These long-legged wasps are reddish-brown or dark brown to black. They have yellow rings on the abdomen, but fewer yellow markings than yellow jackets or hornets. *(See photo on page 70.)*
- They nest near buildings, in meadows and fields, and in gardens on flowers.
- Not as easily riled as yellow jackets and hornets, the paper hornet nevertheless has a painful sting. Paper nests lack outer paper coverings.

Sweat Bee (Halictus spp.)

- The sweat bee's sting is potentially dangerous for those
especially highly allergic and
prone to anaphylactic shock.
Other reactions vary according to number of stings, location of stings, ratio of venom
to body weight, and individual sensitivity. All other factors
being equal, the sting of a
sweat bee is likely the weakest of all bees and wasps.

SWEAT BEE

- Sweat bees are found throughout the United States.
- They are very small, from 0.25 to 0.5 inch.
- Sweat bees are black or brownish, some with greenish or blu-
ish metallic appearance.
- Nests are burrows in clay, in sand banks along streams, and
along roadways or railroad embankments.
- Although there are 502 species of Halictidae in the United States, only about 12 of these are attracted to human
sweat. These sweat bees will sting if they are pressed by
clothing or trapped in the bend of an arm or a leg, but
their sting is not usually very painful and triggers only minor
reactions in normally sensitive individuals. However, in extremely sensitive individuals, the sweat bee sting can trigger anaphylactic shock.

Yellow Jacket (Vespula spp.)

- The yellow jacket's sting is potentially lethal for those highly
allergic and prone to anaphylactic shock. Other reactions vary
according to number of stings, location of stings, ratio of venom to body weight, and individual sensitivity.
- They are found throughout the United States.
- They grow to 0.5 to 0.75 inch.
- The body is yellow and black or black and white. *(See photo
on page 66.)*

{ insects & arachnids }

TYPES OF BEES *(continued)*

Yellow Jacket (continued)

- Yellow jackets are found in woodlands edges, suburban yards, and golf courses. Nests are underground or at ground level in stumps and logs.
- They often appear at picnics in search of food (sweets, meat, and other substances), but do not generally sting at picnics unless accidentally contacted on food. Highly protective of their nests, yellow jackets will sting repeatedly with only slight provocation. Because nests are underground, people most often disturb them with no advance warning.

(continued from page 71)

Getting Rid of Yellow Jacket Nests

Anyone who has angered yellow jackets in a suburban neighborhood will tell you that wasps and people in proximity definitely do not mix. The National Audubon Society's excellent *Field Guide to Insects and Spiders* recommends an apparently low-risk method for ridding your yard of underground yellow jacket nests. At night, place a transparent bowl over the nest opening. Make sure it is set firmly into the ground. When daylight comes, the adults will be confused and unable to escape and seek food. They will not dig a new escape hole and will soon starve to death. Use caution with this method, for yellow jackets will often have a "back door" escape route already in place. If this is the case, you must treat that exit in the same way. Locate these nest openings only by careful observation at the greatest possible distance. While this method seems regrettably cruel (and is untried by the author), it is an alternative

GOOD RIDDANCE

There are many products on the market to help you wipe out individual bees and wasps and their nests, whether they're in the ground, in the trees, under the eaves, or in your wood. Before you tackle a major eradication project, and some folks might think a small, single nest is just such a case, you might want to contact the Cook County agricultural extension agent at (773)768-7779 or a pest control expert for advice on procedures and laws that can affect your choices.

to highly effective chemical treatments and may avert a highly painful and even dangerous event.

If you destroy a yellow jacket nest, it is unlikely that a new colony will take up residence that season. In subsequent years, odds are even that yellow jackets will inhabit the former nest or take up residence elsewhere in your yard or neighborhood.

ANTS

Ants are social insects of the family Formicidae and, along with the related wasps and bees, belong to the order Hymenoptera. Ants evolved from wasp-like ancestors in the mid-Cretaceous period between 110 and 130 million years ago and diversified after the rise of flowering plants. More than 12,500 out of an estimated total of 22,000 species have been classified. They are easily identified by their elbowed antennae and a distinctive node-like structure that forms a slender waist.

Ants form colonies that range in size from a few dozen predatory individuals living in small natural cavities to highly organized colonies that may occupy large territories and consist of millions of individuals. These larger colonies consist mostly of sterile wingless females forming castes of "workers," "soldiers," or other specialized groups. Nearly all ant colonies also have some fertile males called "drones" and one

Black Carpenter Ant
(Camponotus pennsylvanicus)

- The black carpenter ant's bite is painful, but it doesn't sting.
- This ant is common throughout the eastern United States.
- It ranges from 0.25 to 0.5 inch.
- Its body is black, and its enlarged abdomen has long yellow-gray hair.
- It nests in dead wood, including houses, poles, dead tree trunks, and logs.
- This ant is a pest for buildings, but usually only in old wood where it can cause substantial damage.

BLACK ANT

Common Eastern Velvet Ant "Cow Killer" (Dasymutilla occidentalis)

- The sting of the "cow killer" is potentially lethal for those highly allergic and prone to anaphylactic shock. Other reactions vary according to number of stings, location of stings, ratio of venom to body weight, and individual sensitivity.
- It is found in the eastern United States and is common throughout the southeastern United States, becoming more rare in the northern latitudes.
- It grows to 0.5 to 1 inch.
- Its body is covered with long hair-like bristles (setae) of white, orange, red, or black that form patterns.
- This ant is found in meadows, woodland edges, clover fields, and near flowers.
- Eggs are laid in bumblebee nests, and larvae emerge to feed on bee larvae. This is sometimes also called the "red velvet cow killer," but the red velvet ant is actually another related species found in the southwest United States. Neither are true ants, but are actually wasps. Resembling ants in appearance and in movement (plus name), they are included here for easy identification. The sting of workers is reported to be so severe it could "kill a cow." This species is also noted for its speed and ferocity.

VELVET ANT

or more fertile females called "queens." The colonies are sometimes described as super-organisms because the ants appear to operate as a unified entity, collectively working together to support the colony.

Ants have colonized almost every landmass on Earth. The only places lacking indigenous ants are Antarctica and a few remote or inhospitable islands. Ants thrive in most ecosystems, and may form 15–25 percent of the terrestrial animal biomass. Their success in so many environments has been attributed to their social organization and their ability to modify habitats, tap resources, and defend themselves. Their long coevolution with other species has led to their ability to mimic other organisms; form relationships where one organism benefits and the other derives neither benefit nor harm; and live parasitically.

Ant societies have division of labor, communication between individuals, and an ability to solve complex problems. These parallels with human societies have long been an inspiration and subject of study.

Many human cultures make use of ants in cuisine, medication, and rituals. Some species are valued in their role as biological pest control agents. However, their ability to exploit resources brings ants into conflict with humans, as they can damage crops and invade buildings. Some species, such as the red imported fire ant, are regarded as invasive species, establishing themselves in areas where they are accidentally introduced.

If you agitate them enough, most ants are capable of bites and/or stings. The ants profiled here have distinguished themselves for their proclivity to bite or their powerful sting.

LICE

As May R. Berenbaum notes in her fine book, *Bugs in the System: Insects and Their Impact on Human Affairs*, "Life for us humans has probably been lousy ever since we first appeared on the planet." We even have evidence from Egyptian tombs that lice were mummified along with the humans they inhabited, but the relationship almost certainly predates that era. There are two kinds of lice: the biters and the suckers. It's those "little suckers" that find us humans so attractive. In fact, we are host to three types of lice, a rare distinction among mammals.

Hanging by Hairs and Threads

The least harmful, but still irritating, louse lives in pubic hair (but sometimes also in beards, mustaches, and eyebrows), where it can hang on to a single hair for virtually its whole life by its relatively substantial claws.

Hence the nickname "crabs." These lice (Phthirus pubis) are spread during intimate contact, but can survive for a short time off the host, which gives rise to the speculation about the long jump event in the "crab Olympics." Berenbaum gives a smiling nod to nastier bathrooms in this outlandish graffito:

> Don't bother to stretch
> Or stand on the seat.
> The crabs in this place
> Can jump thirty feet.

Symptoms of Pubic Lice
☞ Pubic itching (sometimes in public!)
☞ Visual evidence of lice or nits on pubic hair.

Treatment of Pubic Lice
☞ Apply permethrin 1 percent cream rinse (available without prescription) to affected areas and wash off after ten minutes;
☞ or apply lindane 1 percent shampoo (prescription needed for this generic name, more commonly known as Kwell) for four minutes to the affected area and then thoroughly wash off. This regimen is not recommended for pregnant or lactating women or for children age 2 or younger;
☞ or apply pyrethrins with piperonyl butoxide to the affected area and wash off after ten minutes.

The lindane regimen is the least expensive therapy. Toxicity from lindane has not been reported when treatment was limited to the recommended four-minute period, but use care and follow the directions closely. Permethrin has less potential for toxicity than lindane.

Other Treatment Considerations and Follow-ups
Talk to your pharmacists about other treatment options, and take note of what remedies should not be applied to the eyes. Treat eyelashes by applying ophthalmic ointment to the eyelid margins twice a day for ten days.

Bedding and clothing should be decontaminated (either machine-washed or machine-dried using the heat cycle or dry-cleaned) or removed from body contact for at least 72 hours. Fumigation of living areas is not necessary.

If symptoms persist after one week, retreatment may be necessary if lice are found or if eggs are observed at the hair-skin junction. Patients

who do not respond to one of the recommended regimens should be retreated with an alternative regimen.

Sex partners within the preceding month should be treated.

What Are Head Lice?

They are insects found on the heads of people. Having head lice is very common, and as many as 6 to 12 million people worldwide get head lice each year.

Nit-Picking for Head Lice

Head lice (*Pediculus humanus capitis*), whose eggs are called "nits," mature in about three weeks and tend to infect children, especially those with long hair. With a maximum length of .25 inch, head lice are visible to the human eye, but they are often camouflaged by the fact that they are the color of the hair they inhabit. Infestations can spread rapidly among children in school, but treatment with insecticidal soap and a fine-tooth comb for "nit-picking" usually does the trick.

Who Is at Risk for Getting Head Lice?

Anyone who comes in close contact with someone who already has head lice, or comes in contact with contaminated clothing or other belongings such as combs, brushes, backpacks, or books may be at risk. Preschool and elementary-age children ages 3 to 10 and their families are infested most often. Girls get head lice more often than boys, and women more than men. In the United States, African-Americans rarely get head lice.

{ insects & arachnids }

What Do Head Lice Look Like?

Nits, the eggs, are hard to see and are often mistaken for dandruff or hair spray droplets. Nits are found firmly attached to the hair shaft, are oval, and usually yellow to white for the first 24 hours after being laid, after which they darken to brown. They take about one week to hatch into a nymph that looks like an adult head louse, but is smaller. Nymphs mature into adults about seven days after hatching. To live, the nymph must feed on blood. The adult louse is about the size of a sesame seed, has six legs, and is tan to grayish-white. In persons with dark hair, the adult louse will look darker. Adult lice can live up to 30 days on a person's head. If the louse falls off a person, it dies within two days.

Where Are Head Lice Most Commonly Found?

On the scalp behind the ears and near the neckline at the back of the neck are the most typical places to find head lice. They hold on to hair with hook-like claws at the ends of their six legs, and they are rarely found on the body, eyelashes, or eyebrows.

What Are the Signs and Symptoms of Head Lice Infestation?

☛ Tickling feeling of something moving in the hair.
☛ Itching, caused by an allergic reaction to the bites.
☛ Irritability.
☛ Sores on the head caused by scratching that can sometimes become infected.

How Did My Child Get Head Lice?

By contact with an already infested person through:

☛ Play at school and at home (slumber parties, sports activities, at camp, on a playground).
☛ Wearing infested clothing, such as hats, scarves, coats, sports uniforms, or hair ribbons.
☛ Using infested combs, brushes, or towels.
☛ Lying on a bed, couch, pillow, carpet, or stuffed animal that has recently been in contact with an infested person.

How Do I Diagnose a Head Lice Infestation?

Look closely through the hair and scalp for nits, nymphs, or adults. Finding a nymph or adult may be difficult; there are usually few of them, and they can move quickly from searching fingers. If crawling lice are not seen, finding nits within .25 inch of the scalp confirms that a person is infested and should be treated. If you only find nits more than .25 inch from the scalp, the infestation is probably an old one and does not need to be treated. If you are not sure if a person has head lice, the diagnosis should be made by a health care provider, school nurse, or a professional from the local health department or agricultural extension service.

The Dark Danger of Body Lice

By far, the most potentially dangerous lice are body lice (*Pediculus humanus*), parasitic insects that live on the body and in the clothing or bedding of infested humans (causing a condition called pediculosis). Infestation is common, found worldwide, and affects people of all races. Pediculus can survive in clothing apart from a human host, where they can multiply with astonishing fecundity. One account reported over 10,000 lice and 10,000 nits in a single shirt. Body lice infestations spread rapidly under crowded conditions where hygiene is poor and there is frequent contact among people.

Body lice can produce intense itching, with swelling and skin damage at the site of the bite. This can also bring about a discoloration of the skin in heavy infestations known as "vagabond's disease." In the United States body lice are usually found only in homeless, transient populations who don't have access to changes of clothes or frequent baths. Infestation is unlikely in anyone who bathes regularly.

Can Body Lice Transmit Disease?

Yes. The real danger of body lice is as a carrier of typhus, which can be lethal. Here's how a transmission might occur: Jim has typhus. When a louse feeds on him, the infectious typhus organism Rickettsia kills the louse, but before it dies the louse passes on thousands of pathogens through its feces. The feces dry quickly in the air and easily gain

Pubic Louse (Phthirus pubis)

- Pubic lice cause itching.
- They are found worldwide.
- They grow only to 0.1 inch.
- They have flat, oval, or somewhat elongated gray bodies.
- They live on human bodies in pubic hair, armpit hair, beards, and eyebrows.
- The pubic louse is also known as a "crab louse." It is transmitted only by human-to-human contact because the louse does not leave these cited body regions.

{ insects & arachnids }

entrance to the human body through our moist eyes, noses, or mouth membranes. In another scenario, John, who is not initially infected, can get typhus if he crushes infected lice while scratching them. Then the fecal-carried infection enters John at the point of the bite on his body.

Typhus epidemics often strike where people are forced to live together in crowded, dirty conditions, such as in jail, in refugee camps, or in the military prior to World War II. Historically, typhus has killed many thousands of people worldwide. Although it is a very negligible threat for ordinary folks in North America, the World Health Organization reports it is still endemic in the highlands and cold areas of Africa, Asia, and Central and South America. The onset is often characterized by the sudden appearance of headaches, chills, prostration, high fever, coughing, and severe muscular pain. A macular eruption (dark spot on the skin) appears on the fifth to sixth day, initially on the upper trunk, which then spreads to the entire body excepting, usually, the face, palms, and soles of the feet. Although typhus is now treatable with a single dose of 200 mg of doxycycline, the disease proves fatal for up to 20 percent of those infected.

Where Are Body Lice Found?
Body lice are found on the body and on clothing or bedding used by infested people; lice eggs are laid in the seams of clothing or on bedding. Occasionally eggs are attached to body hair. Lice found on the hair and head are not body lice; they are head lice.

What Are the Signs and Symptoms of Body Lice?
☞ Itching and rash, your body's allergic reaction to the lice, are common.
☞ Long-term body lice infestations may lead to thickening and discoloration of the skin, particularly around the waist, groin, and upper thighs. Sores on the body may be caused by scratching. These sores can sometimes become infected with bacteria or fungi.

How Are Body Lice Spread?
☞ Directly through contact with a person who has body lice.
☞ Indirectly through shared clothing, beds, bed linens, or towels.
☞ It is not possible to contract typhus from either head or pubic lice.

What Do Body Lice Look Like?
There are three forms of body lice: the egg (sometimes called a nit), the nymph, and the adult. Nits are generally easy to see in the seams of

clothing, particularly around the waistline and under armpits. They are about the size of a small ant. Nits may also be attached to body hair. They are oval and usually yellow to white for 24 hours after being laid (after which they darken to brown) and may take 30 days to hatch. The egg hatches into a baby louse called a nymph. It looks like an adult body louse, but is smaller. Nymphs mature into adults about seven days after hatching. To live, the nymph must feed on blood. The adult body louse is about the size of a sesame seed, has six legs, and is tan to grayish-white. Adult lice need to feed on blood to live, and if the louse falls off a person, it dies within ten days.

How Do I Diagnose a Body Lice Infestation?

To locate lice, look closely in the seams of clothing and on the body for eggs and for crawling lice. Diagnosis should be made by a health care provider if you are unsure about infestation.

How Do I Treat a Body Lice Infestation?

Give the infested person a clean change of clothes and a shower, and launder all worn clothing, bed linens, and towels. When laundering items, use the hot cycle (130°F) of the washing machine. Set the dryer to the hot cycle to dry items. Additionally, a 1 percent permethrin or pyrethrin lice shampoo—also called pediculicide (peh-DICK-you-luh-side)—can be purchased at a drugstore without a prescription and then applied to the body. Medication should be applied exactly as directed on the bottle or by your physician.

Human Body Louse
(Pediculus humanus humanus)

- The body louse can transmit typhus.
- It is found worldwide.
- It grows to only 0.1 inch.
- Body lice have flat, oval, or somewhat elongated gray bodies.
- They are found on human bodies, especially in clothing, where they then return to the body to feed on blood.
- The body louse is also known as a "cootie."

BODY LOUSE

{ insects & arachnids }

MOSQUITOES

You've nestled down in a hammock to read, raised your glass to toast the campfire circle, bedded down in the bag to sleep, or crouched in the garden to weed, and then you hear that high, horrible buzzing beside your ear. Damn! The mosquitoes are here!

They are more than an annoyance and more than an itch you want to scratch or smack. Mosquitoes mainline potentially deadly diseases: malaria, yellow fever, dengue, and encephalitis. About the best thing we can say for mosquitoes is that they are a major food source for birds, fish, and bats.

"Pull Out, Betty! You've Hit an Artery!"

Many of us can remember Gary Larson's wonderful *Far Side* cartoon depicting a mosquito that had tapped into a human "gusher" and was about to explode. In fact, female mosquitoes (it's only the females that feed on blood—the males swill only nectar) do "drill" for the blood they use to form eggs. They accomplish this with their proboscis that first "thumps" us, searching for a suitable place to drill. Next, a flexible, knifelike extension, the stylet, pierces the skin and probes under it in several directions in search of a capillary. The mosquito's saliva has an anticlotting protein to induce the blood flow. When our bodies produce histamine to combat this agent, swelling and itching starts.

How Mosquitoes Target Us

The head of a mosquito, it has been said, "bristles with more antennae and sensors than a modern warship." Mosquito eyes can detect motion, as well as assess color and contrast. The head is also equipped to detect carbon dioxide, which is what we exhale. Heat (from our bodies) and lactic acid (from our skin) can also be detected with the insect's headgear. When we wear perfumes and colognes or use fragrant shampoos, soaps, and hair sprays, we beam a strong signal to the girls' many sensors saying, "Eat me!"

When and Where They Are

Short answer: everywhere, almost all the time. From tropical jungles to arctic tundra; from 4,000 feet below sea level in African gold mines to 14,000 feet above sea level in Kashmir; and in all the places in between you'll find one of the 3,200 global species. Not all of these feed on blood, which is a very good thing. If there were more of them that fed on us, we could have even more deadly diseases. Dusk seems to be the preferred time of day for our tiny vampire-like friends, but in marshy areas especially, the sucking never stops.

Encephalitis Frequency, Symptoms, and Treatment

Encephalitis is an inflammation of the brain. Arboviral (insect to human via blood) encephalitides have a global distribution. In the United States, there are six main virus agents of encephalitis that are harmful to humans and domestic animals. In 2010 and early 2011, Cook County saw 30 cases of West Nile virus (one of the six agents), which is transmitted by mosquitoes. Most cases of arboviral encephalitis occur from June through September, when arthropods are most active.

The majority of human infections may lack overt symptoms, or they may result in a nonspecific flu-like syndrome. Onset may be insidious or sudden with fever, headache, myalgias, malaise, and occasionally prostration. Infection may, however, lead to encephalitis, with a fatal outcome or permanent neurological aftereffects. Fortunately, only a small proportion of infected persons progress to full-blown encephalitis.

Because the arboviral encephalitides are viral diseases, antibiotics are not effective for treatment and no effective antiviral drugs have yet been discovered. There are no commercially available human vaccines for these diseases. Treatment is supportive, meaning it attempts to deal with problems such as swelling of the brain, loss of the automatic breathing activity of the brain, and other treatable complications like bacterial pneumonia.

Mosquito Life Cycle

Now that we have a clearer picture of the damage mosquitoes can accomplish with their probing snouts, how can we stop them in their feather-light tracks?

There are 174 different species of mosquitoes in the United States., all of which live in specific habitats and bite different types of animals. Despite these differences, all mosquitoes share some common traits, such as a four-stage life cycle. After the female mosquito obtains a blood meal (male mosquitoes do not bite), she lays her eggs directly on the surface of stagnant water, in a depression, or on the edge of a container where rainwater may collect and flood the eggs. The eggs hatch and a mosquito larva or "wriggler" emerges. The larva lives in the water, feeds, and develops into the third stage of the life cycle called a

{ insects & arachnids }

87

pupa or "tumbler." The pupa also lives in the water, but no longer feeds. Finally, the mosquito emerges from the pupal case and the water as a fully developed adult, ready to bite.

We All Need Water: Interrupting the Life Cycle by Eliminating Mosquito Breeding Sites

All mosquitoes require water to reach adulthood, so the best single thing you can do to reduce mosquitoes around your home is to make sure there is no standing water in which they can reproduce. The best time to hunt for stagnant water is after a rainstorm or after you water the lawn. With diligence you can interrupt the life cycle that produces a new generation of bloodsuckers every 7 to 12 days.

- ☞ Remove containers such as soda cans, tires, buckets, plastic sheeting, or other water catchers from areas surrounding your home.
- ☞ Do not allow water to remain in flowerpot bases or pet dishes for longer than a week.
- ☞ Clean gutters, downspouts, and roofs, to remove leaves and other debris that may hold standing water.
- ☞ Change water in birdbaths and children's wading pools at least once a week.

HOW TO AVOID MOSQUITO BITES

- Stay away from swampy, marshy areas where mosquito populations are high; but if you must go, wear head nets, long sleeves, and long pants. Outdoor specialty stores sell mosquito-proof pants and jackets of tight mesh, with a covering for your entire head.
- Apply repellents, such as DEET or Permanone (containing permethrin) to your clothing, taking care to follow the application instructions. (See more on DEET below.)
- If you don't want to use a DEET-based repellent, look for alternatives such as Avon's Skin-So-Soft, or natural-based applications with lemongrass and pennyroyal. Others in this group include allspice, bay, camphor, cedar, cinnamon, citronella, geranium, lavender, nutmeg, peppermint, pine, and thyme. These may have some repellent properties, but they are limited in effectiveness in comparison to DEET. An extract of eucalyptus oil, though, does have the potential to become a promising alternative to DEET.
- Citronella products, such as candles, provide some help, but if a breeze is blowing their effectiveness is compromised.
- "Backyard foggers" do work temporarily, but like zappers, they are wiping out the good as well as the bad and the ugly, not to mention that you are breathing the deterrent, too.
- Make sure your window and door screens are "bug tight."
- Use yellow "bug lights" outdoors to reduce insect attraction to lighted areas.

☞ Tree holes or stumps can often hold water. Drain them by drilling or fill them with sand or earth.

☞ Water your landscaping so standing water will not accumulate for more than a few days. Fill in any depressions that tend to hold water.

☞ Inspect animal water troughs and the surrounding ground for larval mosquitoes (they look like their name, "wigglers") and change the water if necessary.

☞ Stock your garden pool or ornamental pond with mosquito predators such as the mosquitofish (*Gambusia affinis*) or goldfish.

☞ Check to make sure that covers on boats or pools do not retain water.

☞ Cover rain-collecting barrels with a 16-mesh screen.

Container-breeding mosquitoes usually have a territory of about a city block, so make your cleanup a neighborhood effort with this idea in mind: If it holds water, get rid of it. Dense vegetation serves as resting sites for adult mosquitoes, so trimming it back will help reduce the population, too, as will keeping the grass in check. In *Outwitting Critters: A Humane Guide for Confronting Devious Animals and Winning*, Bill Adler, Jr. advises, "Then there are the bug zappers, which are indiscriminate in their effect, and kill all insects. When you're sitting in the backyard listening to the rapid *zip!* of the zapper, you're hearing good insects go up in smoke. The zapper's light also attracts all the bugs in the neighborhood to your yard. If you want to use a zapper, give one as a present to a neighbor a few houses away."

The Dirt on DEET

DEET (chemical name, diethyl-meta-toluamide) is the active ingredient in many insect-repellent products, and it is used to repel biting pests such as mosquitoes and ticks, including ticks that may carry Lyme disease. Every year in the United States, approximately one-third of the population uses DEET. Products containing DEET currently are available to the public in a variety of liquids, lotions, sprays, and impregnated materials (for example, wristbands, which are of dubious value in repelling insects). Formulations registered with the EPA for direct application to human skin contain from 4 to 100 percent DEET.

DEET is designed for direct application to human skin to repel insects, rather than kill them. After it was developed by the United States Army in 1946, DEET was registered for use by the general public in 1957. As of March 2007, approximately 140 products containing

MOSQUITO
CLOSE-UP

DEET were currently registered with the EPA, down significantly over the previous ten years.

Some people are concerned about the human health implications of using DEET. After evaluation, however, the EPA's regulatory division has concluded that as long as consumers follow label directions and take proper precautions, insect repellents containing DEET do not present a health concern. Part of this evaluation rests on the belief that human exposure is expected to be brief; long-term exposure is not expected. Based on "extensive toxicity testing," the EPA believes that the normal use of DEET does not present a health concern to the general population.

If you are comfortable with going chemical, Dr. Paul Auerbach, healthline.com/health-blogs/outdoor-medicine, has this advice:

Choose a product with one or more of these four active ingredients:
- N,N-diethyl-3-methylbenzamide (DEET)
- butyl 3,4-dihydro-2,2-dimethyl-4-oxo-2H-pyran-6-carboxylate (Indalone)
- 2-ethyl-1,3-hexanediol (EHD; Rutgers 612)
- dimethyl phthalate (DMP)

Good choices include:
- Ben's 100 (100% DEET)
- Cutter spray (18% DEET, 12% DMP)
- Cutter stick (33% DEET), Cutter cream (52% DEET, 13% DMP)
- Muskol spray (25% DEET)
- Muskol lotion (100% DEET)
- OFF! spray (25% DEET)
- Deep Woods OFF! cream (30% DEET)
- Deep Woods OFF! liquid maximum strength (100% DEET)

☞ 6-12 Plus spray (25% EHD, 5% DEET)
☞ Repel spray (40% DEET)

Sawyer Products' Sawyer Product Broad Spectrum Insect Repellent (16.6% DEET plus MGK-264 synergist) is an effective lotion that can be applied to skin to repel ticks, mosquitoes, biting gnats and flies, and fleas. Sawyer Controlled Release Deet Formula is advertised to provide 24-hour protection and to minimize absorption of DEET by using an encapsulating protein to keep the chemical off the skin.

Caution! Do not use repeated applications or concentrations of DEET greater than 15 percent on children under the age of 6 years. In adults, 75 to 100 percent DEET may cause skin rash and, rarely, serious neurological reactions.

Safe Use of DEET Repellents

The following safety regulations from the EPA indicate that although DEET is an effective repellent as a chemical substance, it is nothing to be trifled with.

☞ Do not apply over cuts, wounds, or irritated skin.
☞ Do not apply to hands or near eyes and mouth of young children.
☞ Do not allow young children to apply this product.
☞ Do not use under clothing.
☞ Do not spray in enclosed areas.
☞ Do not spray repellent directly onto face. Spray it on your hands first and then rub it on your face.
☞ Do use just enough repellent to cover exposed skin and/or clothing.
☞ Do avoid breathing a repellent spray and do not use it near food.
☞ Do avoid over-application of this product.
☞ Do wash treated skin with soap and water after returning indoors.
☞ Do wash treated clothing before wearing it again.

Use of DEET may cause skin reactions in rare cases. If you suspect an adverse reaction, discontinue use of the product, wash treated skin, and call your local poison control center or physician for help. If you go to a doctor, take the repellent container with you.

Children and Insects

☞ Apply an insect repellent regularly to the child's skin if in an area where bites are a risk (note that repellents are not effective against stinging insects). Use a repellent with the lowest possible concentration of DEET or use a natural repellent without DEET.
☞ Dress the child in light-colored clothing thick enough that insects can't bite through it.

{ insects & arachnids }

91

House Mosquito (Culex pipiens)

- This mosquito is a carrier for West Nile Virus, a type of encephalitis.
- It is found in many countries of the world.
- It is .25 to .5 inch long.
- The house mosquito is light brown.
- It is a city dweller that lives near people but mostly feeds on birds. This probably accounts for its West Nile virus vector identity.
- It breeds in almost any water container and prefers polluted water.

☞ Teach the child to be respectful of bugs' homes: this may mean not turning over rocks and logs (or doing so carefully and only with adult supervision), and not disturbing spider webs.

☞ Teach the child to shake out shoes and clothing before putting them on, especially if the shoes and clothes have been sitting outdoors.

☞ Teach the child to freeze ("play statue") when he or she is being investigated by stinging insects so that the child doesn't frighten the insect into stinging.

☞ Keep tent screens zipped, opening them only to enter and exit the tent.

☞ Have the child sleep enclosed in a mosquito net if in an area where mosquitoes are especially numerous or persistent.

☞ Shake out the child's sleeping bag or bedding before going to sleep. Have the child wear shoes at all times, especially after dark when insects are likely to be around.

☞ Coating the skin with mud, something children might enjoy, also acts as a repellent.

☞ Apply repellent to children yourself so that it doesn't get on their hands or in their mouths or eyes. Keep repellent off of a child's hands so they don't rub it in their eyes or get it in their mouths.

☞ Do not apply insect repellent to infants.

☞ Do not apply insect repellent underneath clothing.

☞ Wash insect repellent off of the skin after bites are no longer a threat.

Public Spraying to Control Mosquitoes

If you live in areas where massive mosquito control has become a governmental concern, you may occasionally have ULV (Ultra Low Volume) spray trucks rumble through your neighborhood, spreading a

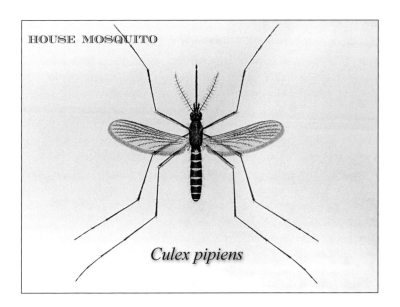

HOUSE MOSQUITO

Culex pipiens

chemical repellent, or maybe your pesticide is delivered via airmail. The EPA has evaluated the risks of human exposure to these compounds such as malathion and naled, and has determined them to be from 100 to 10,000 times below an amount that would pose a health concern. Their estimates projected several spraying events over a period of weeks and factored in the assumption that a toddler would eat some soil and grass during that interval, too. Although the EPA is not worried about your overexposure to such compounds, they do recommend the following:

- ☞ Listen and watch for announcements about spraying and remain indoors during the application in your area.
- ☞ If you have chemical sensitivities or think the spraying might aggravate an existing health problem, contact you doctor or your local health department to take special measures to avoid exposure.
- ☞ Close your windows and turn off window air conditioners when spraying is taking place.
- ☞ Do not let children play near truck-mounted applicators when they are in use.

Because mosquitoes do not vary widely in appearance and because the house mosquito is responsible for transmitting West Nile virus found in Cook County, I depict only this species although other mosquitoes are found in Illinois.

{ insects & arachnids }

FLIES

"Wouldn't hurt a fly," the saying goes, but if you've had big or little buzzing biters attack you, it's easy to wonder where in the world that saying originated. Flies belong to the Diptera ("two winged") order, the group of insects with one pair of flight wings. However, they do have a second pair of "wings"—knobby organs used for flight stability called halteres. North America has about 16,300 of the world's 86,000 known species, with many still awaiting discovery. Thousands of species are known only from fossils, the oldest of which, a Limoniidae crane fly, is some 225 million years old. Members of the order Diptera include mosquitoes and midges as well as flies.

Flies are so commonplace you'd have to go to the Arctic poles to escape them. They destroy our food, especially grains and fruits, and they can also be superior disease carriers, as well as aggravating biters, depending on the species. On the positive side, they are important in pollination and as a food supply for other animals. On the dark positive side, the blue bottle fly or common blowfly (Calliphora vomitoria) keeps wounds sterile while they feed upon them, but they do retard healing. (Surprise!)

Low Life

You've seen them land on your sandwich, but try not to think about where those fly feet have been before that. It's as bad as you think it is: flies subsist on various organic substances including excrement. This makes them transmitters of germs for infectious diseases such as cholera, dysentery, diarrhea, typhoid fever, salmonellosis, hepatitis, and poliomyelitis.

Most fly species reproduce in dry areas, with breeding promoted by warm temperatures, so summertime is party time for flies. They lay up to 2,000 eggs, mostly in manure, feces, compost heaps, and some species deposit them on protein-rich substances such as meat. These eggs grow to become white maggots, larvae typical of the Diptera order that are soft, legless, and look headless. Probably to your horror, you may have discovered them in the cat litter box in summer if you were negligent in freshening it. If you don't tightly secure and cover your garbage, you'll also offer the best possible habitat for flies to reproduce. Consider that they can complete their development in 7 to 14 days, and it's a quick turnaround to an out-of-control fly problem.

There is good reason to reduce the fly population. Adult houseflies, for example, feed on a wide range of liquid waste but can eat solid foods, such as sugar. To digest solid foods, houseflies liquefy food by regurgitating. During feeding, they also defecate on the food. No wonder then that each housefly can easily carry over one million bacteria on its body. They are passive transmitters of disease, carrying pathogens that "hitch a ride" on their bodies.

To Prevent Passive Disease Transmission by Flies:
☛ Cover food as much as possible on picnics.
☛ Eliminate breeding areas such as garbage piles and spilled animal feed.
☛ Bury all dead animals.
☛ Compost carefully, being sure never to put animal feces, meat scraps, or other animal products in a compost pile.

Biting Flies
Other varieties of flies, such as deerflies and horseflies, spread trouble by biting to feed on small amounts of blood from several animals in succession. The biters are almost always the females in search of a protein meal needed to carry on the reproduction of the species. As it is with mosquitoes, every time a biting fly takes a blood meal it injects a small amount of salivary fluid to help prevent coagulation within and around its mouthparts. This fluid contains proteins that act as allergens, resulting in swollen, itchy welts. A more generalized anaphylactic reaction, though fortunately rare, can occur in a few individuals who are hypersensitive. Some species of biting flies seem to have more allergenic saliva than others. Blackflies may be worse than others in this regard.

American horseflies and deerflies may also transmit bacteria that cause tularemia, an infection transferred from an animal to a human that is most often transmitted by ticks and rabbits. Normally, it is not possible to catch the disease from other humans. Biting flies have also been linked to the transmission of anthrax, but this is so rare in the United States that your chances of contamination by biting flies are virtually nonexistent.

Blackflies
Also known as buffalo gnats and turkey gnats, blackflies are small, bloodsucking insects slightly less than .25 inch long with a stout body and hump-backed appearance. They are much more of a pest in the northern reaches of the United States, like Illinois, but they are found as far south as Florida. Legendary for their bite, blackflies have piercing and sucking mouthparts similar to those of mosquitoes. Thanks to wing beats of around 300 times per second, mosquitoes will warn you of their presence, but blackflies are like stealth bombers. Typically several will hover maddeningly around your head while they take turns striking. They are prone to strike out of your range of vision—behind

{ insects & arachnids }

Blackfly (Simulium spp.)

- The blackfly has a painful bite.
- It is found throughout the eastern United States south to Florida but is more common in northern latitudes.
- It grows to 0.1 to 0.2 inch.
- It is stout, black or dark brown with short antennae, humped thorax, and short legs.
- The blackfly is found close to running water in forests and mountains.
- It is also called buffalo gnat or turkey gnat. It carries a parasitic worm in other parts of the world that causes blindness, but is not a vector for disease in the United States. Worst bites occur in late spring and early summer.

your ears, on your scalp, or inside your collar. Though they favor the head just beneath the hat rim, all exposed parts of the body are subject to attack. Blackfly bites are bigger than mosquito bites, and they sometimes bleed due to anticoagulants in the insects' saliva, and these bites itch longer and more persistently. Livestock, pets, poultry, and wildlife are also severely irritated by these flies.

Their biting season occurs in spring and early summer just as the weather tempts humans outside. Their numbers, as well as their tendency to bite, increases as sunset approaches, but they do not bite after dark. Some species of blackfly females, fresh from their underwater cocoons in cold streams, must have blood (from mammals or birds) to create their eggs—a system that is 180 million years old. Other phases of their life cycles pose no imposition on humans or on other mammals whatsoever.

Although there are cases of blackfly bites inducing anaphylactic shock, the vast majority of bites are merely aggravating, and in the United States, blackflies are not known to transmit diseases to humans.

Beyond lack of disease transmission, blackflies offer another plus as described by Stewart Edward White in his 1903 book, *The Forest*:

. . . [The blackfly is to be complimented because] he (sic) holds still to be killed. No frantic slaps, no waving of arms, no muffled curses. You just place your finger calmly and firmly on the spot. You get him every time. In this is great, heart lifting joy. It may be unholy joy, perhaps even vengeful, but it leaves the spirit ecstatic. The satisfaction of murdering the beast that has had the nerve to light on you just as you are reeling in, almost counter-balances the pain. . . .

Signs of Blackfly Bites
☞ Punctures that may bleed.
☞ Immediate pain, swelling (welt), and redness that is frequently intense and persistent.
☞ Sores that may persist for weeks.
☞ Multiple bites can produce swollen lymph glands, particularly in children.

Avoiding Blackfly Bites
☞ Avoid areas along rivers and streams during late spring and early summer, though blackflies cross hills and may be found miles from their lowland breeding sites.
☞ Take refuge indoors or in a car. When trapped inside something, blackflies concentrate on escape, not on feeding.
☞ Tuck pants cuffs into your socks and button shirts up. Blackflies can-not bite through clothing, but they will crawl under it to bite in such aggravating spots as the ankles and waist.
☞ Wear light-colored clothing such as white or yellow.
☞ Avoid blue, purple, brown, and black clothing.
☞ Blue jeans without holes that are tucked into socks might be better than pale trousers because they may attract the flies away from your head.
☞ Use insect repellents. Spraying a DEET-based repellent on your jacket will likely discourage most blackflies from crawling under your shirt or into your hair.

Sue Hubbell, a fine writer and beekeeper by trade, discovered that a nylon (not cotton) bee suit with a zippered veil and cowhide gloves are just right for heavy blackfly season in Maine during the months of May and June. It might be worth a try, though note that nylon won't absorb DEET.

Deerflies and Horseflies
Both of these biters will feed on humans, but it's more likely a deerfly that's biting you, and more likely a horsefly that's after your livestock.

{ insects & arachnids }

Both generally resemble a housefly, but the deerfly is slightly larger than a housefly, and the horsefly can start to take on sci-fi proportions when they reach over an inch in length. Deerflies come in late spring-early summer. Horseflies are more of a late summer phenomenon. Both types of flies are potential vectors of such diseases as anthrax, tularemia, anaplasmosis, hog cholera, equine infectious anemia, and filariasis, and perhaps Lyme disease, according to the *New England Journal of Medicine* in 1990.

Not a delicate date at all, the deerfly rams her sharp, knifelike jaws into your skin, leaving no doubt she has arrived for that blood Slurpee she craves to get her reproductive wheels spinning. The bite is painful and can leave a mark of blood after feeding on humans, cattle, horses, mules, hogs, dogs, deer, and other warm-blooded animals. The anticoagulant they inject to keep the blood flowing triggers our histamines that causes the stinging response to their bites.

Miniature female winged vampires, adult deerflies emerge from the soil in late May or early June, ready to rock and roll. They frequently attack humans along summer beaches, near streams, and at the edges of moist, wooded areas. Some people, when bitten, suffer severe lesions, high fever, and even general disability. These symptoms are allergic reactions to hemorrhagic saliva poured into the wound to prevent clotting while the fly is feeding. A person can become increasingly sensitive to repeated bites.

Deerfly and Horsefly Bites

- ☞ They are more likely to occur on warm, sunny days when there is little or no wind.
- ☞ They are less likely to occur when the temperature drops slightly or when a breeze arises.
- ☞ They can be repelled with DEET-based solutions carefully applied according to instructions, although permethrin-based repellents applied only on clothing usually last longer.
- ☞ Mesh jackets treated with repellents that slip on over regular outdoor clothing can be very effective when a strong repellent is applied. Store the jacket in a sealed plastic bag.
- ☞ Gloves offer good protection.
- ☞ Buttoned-up and tightly woven, long-sleeved shirts and long pants can also help.
- ☞ Light-colored clothing is preferred to dark.
- ☞ Area repellents with citronella or naphthalene are helpful to repel deerflies and mosquitoes in or near a patio, yard, tent, or cabin.
- ☞ Providing daytime shelter for humans and animals is important, as horseflies and deerflies do not appear to bite much at night.

American Horsefly (*Tabanus americanus*)

- Their bites are painful with remote chances of transmission of tularemia.
- They are found throughout the United States east of the Rocky Mountains.
- They grow to .75 to 1.25 inches.
- The horsefly's body is large and broad with a brown-black thorax and dark red-brown abdomen. Wings are smoky. Eyes are large and green.
- They are found near standing water such as ponds, marshes, and swamps.
- According to Ross H. Arnett, Jr. "The Declaration of Independence was signed July 4, 1776, instead of a later date that would have permitted further discussion because the horseflies in Philadelphia were biting so fiercely at the time that the delegates decided to adjourn just to get away from them." (Arnett, 2000, p. 870)
- After being quickly sliced by knifelike mouthparts and receiving an anticoagulant via saliva, horsefly wounds may continue to bleed. Repeated attacks may cause serious weakening of livestock due to loss of blood.

HORSEFLY

{ insects & arachnids }

Deerfly (Chrysops spp.)

- Its painful bite has a remote chance of transmitting tularemia.
- It is found throughout the United States.
- It is 0.25 to 1 inch.
- Wings have distinctive brownish-black pattern. Body is black with yellow-green markings.
- The deerfly is found in damp woodlands, suburbs near water, meadows, and roadsides, especially with standing water.
- This fly is active from May to September. It can be distinguished from horseflies, which have either clear or black wings or very small markings.

DEERFLY

Deerfly Bites
☞ Deerflies seem to be attracted to moving objects and dark shapes.
☞ Bites are likely to occur around the face and neck.
☞ As many as four to five flies may simultaneously attack.

Horsefly Bites
☞ Horseflies are usually attracted to shiny surfaces, motion, carbon dioxide, and warmth.
☞ Horseflies may attack while you are swimming in a pool.

Housefly (Musca domestica)

- These are mechanical transmitters of typhoid fever, dysentery, pinworms, hookworms, tapeworms, and salmonella.
- They are found worldwide.
- They range from 0.1 to 0.25 inch.
- The housefly has red eyes and clear wings on a gray body with four black stripes on the thorax.
- They are found on exposed or rotting food and manure.
- These are aptly named, as 98 percent of flies in your house are houseflies.

HOUSEFLY

Treatment for Fly Bites
☞ Take oral antihistamines, such as Benadryl.
☞ Apply ice to affected areas.

Controlling Flies
☞ Do not accumulate piles of garbage and rotting substances where flies will eat and breed.
☞ Do not leave food or meals uncovered.
☞ Do keep kitchens and cooking utensils clean.
☞ Do use insect repellents to provide effective protection against biting flies.

Bed Netting Protection
Horseflies, blackflies, sand flies, deerflies, gnats, and other assorted nuisances may not be driven away by insect repellents. At such times, fashion has to fall by the wayside, and a head net (not a hair net) may be invaluable during times of high mosquito infestation. Netting can be an excellent defense, especially at night. If you use a bed net, be certain that it is free of holes and has its edges tucked in. The net needs to be woven to a tightness of 18 threads per inch (6 to 7 per centimeter). Tighter mesh may hinder ventilation, and a net that has been dipped in an insecticide, usually permethrin, is more effective. Note that fleas and chiggers are generally not deterred by bed nets.

{ insects & arachnids }

MIDGES

No-see-ums

Biting midges of the Ceratopogonidae family are also called sand flies, no-see-ums, punkies, mouse flies, and flying teeth. The smallest of the biting flies, less than 0.25 inch long, they look (under a microscope) like short-legged mosquitoes. They are so small you probably won't be aware of them until they have started to feed on you. They can be very annoying, leaving a painful red bump that seems out of proportion to their size. After your immune system becomes sensitized to these bites, reactions may become worse. After repeated assaults you may develop blisters or small sores. As usual, it's the females that are feeding on you, but not all biting midges go after humans. Some feed on other insects, pollen, and nectar.

No-see-ums live most often near salt marshes, ponds, or streams, and by some accounts they stay within 100 yards or so of their breeding area where their eggs are laid in gelatinous masses on the water surface. So, the farther you can get from the water source, the less likely you are to be bitten. That, plus insect repellent, is about your only line of defense against them.

Biting Midge (Culicoides spp.)

- Their bite is severe and their numbers can be overwhelming.
- They are found throughout the United States.
- Quite small, they are generally 0.1 to 0.2 inch long.
- Midges resemble tiny blackflies.
- They are found near water, in wet soil, both sandy and clay soil, streambeds with moist decaying vegetation, and marshy areas, particularly those contaminated with animal sewage.
- Midges are considered a serious local pest. Most attacks occur around dusk, on cloudy days, or in shaded areas because females are only active in low light.

BITING MIDGE

CATERPILLARS

One of the great romantic stories of nature is how the lowly "worm" transforms into a spectacular, ephemeral paradigm of grace, beauty, and flight. Of course, this is the story of the metamorphosis of butterflies and moths, which begin life as eggs and then become caterpillars. After shedding their skins, these caterpillars either spin a cocoon if they are to evolve into a moth, or find a safe hiding place if they are to become a butterfly. A final skin shedding reveals the pupa (from the Latin for girl or doll), an outer shell with no head or feet. Inside this shell the final metamorphosis into a winged wonder will occur.

During the larval stage, a caterpillar is a creature with a mission: eat, survive, and transform. As a part of its protective equipment, some caterpillars possess stinging spines or hairs. These sharp spines are hollow and sometimes connected to venom glands (venom flows on contact), or, similar to glass fibers, the hairs break off and lodge in skin easily, causing pain like a needle prick.

Individual reactions to these "stings" vary from mild discomfort (itching, redness, swelling, and a raised rash) to severe pain. At the extreme end, some people may experience severe swelling, nausea, and generalized systemic reactions, occasionally requiring hospital treatment. In some cases, entrance of hairs into the eye can cause blindness.

Just touching a hairy or spiny caterpillar can cause skin irritation, so wash well with soap and water after contact with a caterpillar, and don't touch your eyes, nose, or mouth until you do.

Avoiding Caterpillar Stings

Stings (we'll use the term for convenience, though caterpillar spines are not true stingers) generally occur when people accidentally brush against one of these caterpillars or when they attempt to remove it by hand from clothing or the body. Interactions usually occur in summer or obviously whenever the species is in the larval stage. Caterpillars are often found on leaves, vegetable plants, shrubs, and trees, and they are often encountered when harvesting sweet corn in late summer and early autumn. Wear long-sleeve shirts, trousers, and gloves when gathering the ears to reduce possible stings. When among trees, caterpillars may drop down on you. Here's a story:

> *When Trent was canoeing in North Carolina, he leaned forward to paddle under some overhanging trees. He felt something tickle down his back under his shirt, but at the time the rocks and the rapids had more of his attention. When he was able to stop, he found a caterpillar inside his shirt. He rid himself of the creature, but did not*

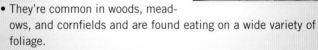

Io Moth Caterpillar (Automeris io)

- Their spines can penetrate skin to cause a painful sting.
- They are found across the eastern United States.
- They grow to 3 inches long.
- These caterpillars are green with reddish and white side stripes. Body segments have clumps of spines.
- They're common in woods, meadows, and cornfields and are found eating on a wide variety of foliage.
- They spin cocoons in ground debris.

IO MOTH CATERPILLAR

try to wash his back, sensing no immediate overt reaction. By that evening, however, the allergic response to the caterpillar's venom had taken effect. Several days later Trent was fine, but in the meantime he had swelling, a rash, and enough muscle soreness to make turning his head difficult. If he had been able to wash his back, or even rinse it, and perhaps apply ice when the swelling began, his caterpillar incident might have been less severe.

Be careful when attempting to brush caterpillars off. Never swat or crush by hand. Remove them carefully and slowly with a stick or other object. Never handpick these hairy, fuzzy, or spiny caterpillars except with heavy leather gloves if necessary.

Individuals, especially children, should be cautioned about handling or playing with any colorful, hairy, fuzzy caterpillars since it is sometimes difficult to distinguish between harmless and venomous insect larvae. To be on the safe side, tell them if it is hairy or fuzzy and looks like a teeny, tiny hot dog, leave it alone.

Treatment for Caterpillar Stings

Diagnosis is usually simple since a rash generally breaks out where the hairs or spines have made skin contact.

☞ Immediately apply and then remove adhesive or transparent tape over the sting site to remove broken hairs or spines. Repeat as necessary.

Saddleback Moth Caterpillar (*Sibine stimulea*)

- Spines cause sting on contact.
- These caterpillars are found in the eastern United States.
- They grow to 1 inch.
- It has a brilliant green body with dark brown ends and a highly distinctive dark brown oval, or "saddle," on its back encircled with white. It also has tufts of hairs (spines) along body sides.

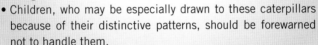

SADDLEBACK CATERPILLAR

- This caterpillar is found in gardens, woods edges, and orchards where it feeds on a wide variety of foliage.
- Children, who may be especially drawn to these caterpillars because of their distinctive patterns, should be forewarned not to handle them.

☛ Wash the affected skin area thoroughly with soap and water. This may help remove irritating venom.

☛ Promptly apply an ice pack and a baking-soda poultice to help reduce pain and swelling.

☛ Household analgesics, such as aspirin, are not very effective in reducing pain and headache, but an oral antihistamine such as Benadryl may help relieve itching and burning.

☛ Topical corticosteroids may reduce the intensity of inflammatory reaction.

☛ Desoximetasone gel, a prescription topical steroid, applied twice daily to affected areas will help.

☛ Contact a physician promptly if severe reactions occur.

☛ Very young, aged, or unhealthy persons are more likely to suffer severe reaction symptoms.

{ insects & arachnids }

TRUE BUGS

So what's a true bug? An old VW? Actually, entomologists (those people whom Gary Larson regularly skewered in his *Far Side* cartoons as half-wits) really do have an order called "true bugs," or Hemiptera, which means "half wing." True bugs have forewings called hemelytra, leathery

Bed Bug (*Cimex lectularius*)

- Bed bugs bite. They have been implicated as disease carriers, but this has not been proven.
- They can be found throughout the United States.
- They are only 0.2 inch long.
- Flat and reddish brown to purplish with short legs and stubby (vestigial) wings.
- They can be found in human dwellings, especially bedrooms, in all socioeconomic classes.
- Each feeding bug makes several punctures. As the bugs' salivary fluid is not immediately irritating, their bites can go unnoticed for a period of time. After feeding, the nymphs and adults hide to be out of harm's way and can survive up to 15 months without food.

BED BUG

Bloodsucking Conenose (*Triatoma sanguisuga*)

- Bites can cause severe allergic reactions.
- These are found from New Hampshire south to Florida and west as far as Texas.
- They are 0.5 to 0.75 inch long.
- They are black to dark brown with yellow-red markings (six spots).
- They are found in small animal nests and may invade houses.
- They feed on bed bugs, humans, and other mammals. Also known as the "Mexican bed bug or the big bed bug.

BLOODSUCKING CONENOSE

Wheel Bug (*Arilus cristatus*)

- The wheel bug can "stab" when handled. Its bite usually is more severe than a bee sting, and both nymphs and adults should be avoided or handled with caution.
- It has been reported from Rhode Island westward through Iowa and Nebraska to California, and southward to Texas and Florida
- It is 1 to 1.25 inches.
- The adult is black to grayish-brown. Nymph is deep red with black markings. The name derives from the semicircular arrangement of 8 to 12 tubercles (small, knoblike projections) resembling half a wheel.
- It is found in meadows and fields with crops.
- The perceived "stab" is actually a bite.

WHEEL BUG

thick in the front, and transparent and membranous in the back. Another way to identify true bugs is by the way they fold their wings flat over their bodies, making an X-shape. They have sucking beaks to slurp juices, but most feed on plants. Another common trait is that most true bugs also have glands that dispatch a foul odor, e.g., the green stink bug. Most true bugs are terrestrial, but some are aquatic and can literally walk on water.

The insects we're concerned with here are in the assassin bug family (Reduviidae). They bite you in defense or in search of a blood meal. Assassin bugs are named for the way they attack and "stab" victims, which is actually a bite. Chicago has its share of assassins, notably bed bugs.

IF YOU ARE BITTEN BY A BUG
- Wash the bite with soap and water.
- Apply topical relief such as Benadryl ointment, and/or
- Take Benadryl orally if a stronger reaction such as increased swelling occurs.
- Bug bites are not known for producing anaphylactic shock, but it's always a good idea to monitor reactions of any encounter for the first hour or two.

{ insects & arachnids }

SPIDERS

Perhaps spiders can generate such strong responses in us because they loom large in our symbolic understanding of the world. In Egyptian, Babylonian, Greek, Norse, Hindu, Buddhist, Japanese, Oceanic, African, Caribbean, and Native American cultures, to name a few, the creature that is smaller than a human hand and usually about the size of a penny or less, has held a revered position for millennia. In myth, spiders are portrayed as no less than the Great Mother, the great weaver of fate, the creator of the world who spins the thread of life from her body and attaches humanity to it, binding people together as one. The core of her web is the cosmic hub, whose rays, like the sun, extend outward to life.

A Shy Personality and a Killer Body

Maybe it happens in your dreams, but in reality spiders will not chase you. (Jumping spiders can leap 20 times their own length to capture food, but they are not going to make a flying leap at a human.) In fact, spiders as a whole are seldom aggressive, generally biting only when threatened or injured. They do bite when ordering dinner, but we're not on their menu. They are interested in liquified flies and other similar arachnid culinary delights, and they down many pounds of mostly insects every year. Even if they did want to turn the tables on us and wrap their tiny little mouths around our big succulent thighs, with a few important exceptions, the low-level toxicity of their venom is negligible for humans.

Spiders are most easily recognized by their four pairs of legs divided into seven segments. Like other arachnids, spiders possess a cephalothorax and abdomen, but they also have a "waist" or pedicel, a body configuration that scorpions, mites, and daddy longlegs do not possess. Although variety among spiders is great, most have eight simple, not compound, eyes that are in two or three rows. Below the eyes are two small jaws, the chelicerae, that end in fangs. Venom produced in these glands empties into the fangs through a duct. That venom is released when spiders want to paralyze or kill prey.

How Do Spiders Prey?

Silently. Almost all spiders are poisonous, or, more accurately, venomous. This means they bite their victims and inject venom that essentially breaks down the prey so that the spider can then eat it in its "predigested" form, though what happens next varies. Most spiders then puncture the insect's exoskeleton, pump in that digestive enzyme that liquifies the "innards," and then suck that soup right into their stomachs, leaving just a mere shell of what once was probably a viable six-legger. Other spiders use their jaws to grind their prey to a pulp before they spray it with digestive juices and then suck it up.

Which Spiders Have Dangerous Bites?

Many spiders do bite, but for the most part their bites are insignificant. However, just as bee and wasp stings may trigger allergic reactions in some people, the same can be true for spider bites. Young children, the elderly, and hypersensitive individuals are more likely to react strongly to a spider bite. Encounters between people and spiders are usually accidental and occur when the spider's web or nest is disturbed. There are 3,000 spider species in North America, but only black widows, recluses, hobos, and tarantulas are chief causes for concern. In Chicago worry only about black widows and yellow sac spiders. Generally speaking, black widows make you ill overall, and yellow sacs affect the tissue at the bite site, perhaps turning it necrotic.

Reducing Spider Populations

Spiders are overwhelmingly beneficial creatures, and we owe them gratitude for eating the many insects that feed on the flowers, shrubs, and other plants in our gardens and natural areas. Many folks, however, still just don't want them in the general vicinity. Keep in mind, though, that if you spray chemicals to reduce general spider populations, you may actually increase your number of pests by also destroying the spider's natural enemies.

DARING JUMPING SPIDER

{ insects & arachnids }

109

Although not all spiders build webs (some hide and some just hang out), web-building spiders are most likely to show up in areas where insects are abundant: for example, around wood-piles, porch lights, windows, or water sources such as spigots. (In the

WOLF SPIDER

end, it's always about food and water.) Knocking down these webs with a broom or burst of water from a garden hose will provide adequate regulation. Outdoor pesticide applications for spiders are largely unnecessary and should be avoided.

On occasion, you will find spiders on objects or in areas that have been left undisturbed, including sandboxes or even children's toys. Check these items periodically for signs of spiders. For obvious reasons, don't spray pesticides around sandboxes or other play areas unless you absolutely must.

Likewise, if you have spiders indoors, that means they are getting the survival substances they need, such as insects. If you work to reduce the insects, the spider population in your house will decline, too.

You can also:

☞ Knock down webs.

☞ Vacuum along baseboards, in corners, and under furniture.

☞ Clean bookshelves periodically.

If you're concerned that more spiders will show up (or hatch from an unseen egg sac), then you could resort to applying an insecticide along baseboards, in corners, and inside storage closets, but be sure to select a pesticide that is labeled for use against spiders indoors. Always read the insecticide label for complete instructions on how and where to use the product.

Treating your crawl space is an option, but exercise extreme caution when applying pesticides in such confined areas without adequate ventilation and personal protection. For these reasons crawl space treatments are often best left to pest control professionals. The Cook County agricultural extension agent at (733) 768-7779 can advise you on the latest and wisest methods for large-scale problems.

What to Do If You Think You Have Been Bitten by a Venomous Spider

☛ Remain calm. The chances that your wound will be fatal are extremely remote.

☛ Carefully apply ice or a cold pack to decrease pain, though ice should not be applied directly to the skin.

☛ Collect the specimen, if possible, for a positive identification. If you can't easily do this, do try to get a good look at the spider, and if possible get a family member, neighbor, coworker, or friend working on the identification, too.

☛ Seek medical attention or contact your local poison control center immediately.

Chicago Area Poison Resource Center
Medical Center
1753 West Congress Parkway
Chicago, IL 60612
(312) 942-5969

AAPCC Certified
Illinois Poison Center
222 South Riverside Plaza, Suite 1900
Chicago, IL 60606
Emergency Phone: (800) 222-1222; (312) 906-6185 (TTY/TDD)

☛ *You may also call a national hotline, (800) 222-1222, and you will be connected to the center that serves your area.*

Before calling emergency facilities, determine the following information:

☛ Patient's age, weight, and condition.
☛ Time the bite occurred.
☛ Area where the bite occurred.
☛ Identity of the spider, if possible.

Poison Control will help you determine what steps to take next.

{ insects & arachnids }

GENERAL RULES FOR AVOIDING SPIDER BITES

• Check for spiders before sticking your bare hands into dark corners or areas.
• Wear work gloves when handling boxes, firewood, lumber, and other items that have been stored/stacked undisturbed for some time.
• Before wearing stored clothing, shake vigorously to dislodge any spiders and inspect it carefully.

If I Am Bitten, How Serious Will the Bite Be?

The answer to this question depends on

- ☞ Species of spider.
- ☞ Area of the body where the bite occurs.
- ☞ Amount of venom injected.
- ☞ Depth of the bite.

Black Widow Spiders

The intrigue of it all: "She mates, she bites, he dies, and now she is . . . the widow. . . the black widow of death!" Sounds like a promo for a Hitch-cock horror movie, doesn't it? Indeed, many people do find the thought of black widow spiders spine-tingling. They are probably one of the first "deadly" creatures that children learn about, coloring the coal black bod-ies and the infamous "reddish-orange hourglass" on their bellies. In the Chicago-area northern black widow, the distinctive "hour glass" marking on the underside of the abdomen is split in the middle. Northern widows also have a series of red spots along the dorsal midline of the abdomen, and many have a series of lateral white stripes on the abdomen.

The male is shy and rarely seen by humans, and although the female does attack the male after he has fulfilled his reproductive duties, this does not happen in every case. Of course, they kill other creatures in search of food, but females are generally not aggressive unless they perceive a threat or are guarding an egg sac.

The black widow female builds a large, stout, funnel-shaped web. She hangs upside down in front of the funnel, displaying her vivid col-oration to potential predators. The spider senses a vibration in the web when prey happens upon it. Then she moves swiftly toward the prey, throwing a sticky, viscous entangling silk. With the prey thus immobi-lized, the black widow bites to inject the potent, paralyzing neurotoxin. In this way the black widow spider consumes not only insects, centi-pedes, and other small invertebrates, but also prey that are proportion-ately much larger, such as giant cockroaches and small gecko lizards. The black widow itself is vulnerable to predators—primarily birds, Ano-lis lizards, and jumping spiders.

Why Do They Bite?

Normally, the black widow will curl up into a ball and drop to the ground if she has nowhere to run, defensive only if she is guarding her egg sac. Otherwise black widows are shy by nature and bite only when trapped or sat on.

Northern Black Widow Spider (*Latrodectus variolus*)

- The black widow bite is potentially lethal, but fatalities are rare.
- It is common throughout most of the United States.
- The body is 0.3 inch long.
- The female (biter) body is black. The spherical abdomen has a red hourglass pattern on its underside that is broken into two parts. Many also have a series of lateral white stripes on the abdomen.
- The black widow web is funnel-shaped, with an irregular weave, and is found in sheltered sites.
- Black widows can be found in dark and damp areas such as among fallen branches and under any object (inside or out) likely to trap moisture, such as trash.
- Probably the most feared spider, the black widow will attempt to escape rather than bite unless it is guarding an egg mass.

NORTHERN BLACK WIDOW SPIDER

{ insects & arachnids }

How to Avoid Black Widow Bites

Black widows can be found almost anywhere in the Western hemisphere. The key words are "dark" and "damp" places.

Their favorite spots outside are:

- Woodpiles
- In dense plant growth
- Trash piles
- Fruit and vegetable gardens
- Under rocks
- In electrical, water, and telephone equipment boxes

- Under boards
- Tree stumps
- Storage sheds
- Stone walls
- In drainage pipes
- In sheds, barns, well houses, and root cellars

Although they are not as prevalent as they once were, outhouses are another legendary place for black widows, where the genitals seem especially vulnerable. Curiously, some sources say not even urinating men are exempt. (Makes you want to wait until you get home, doesn't it?)

Their favorite places inside are:

- Closets
- Garages
- Crawl spaces
- Beneath appliances

- Under furniture
- Inside boxes
- Storage sheds
- Inside seldom-worn shoes

To reduce your chances of a bite:

- Discourage your children from playing in rock piles or woodpiles.
- If you are working outside in the yard in big piles of logs or leaves, wear gloves.
- Shake out blankets and clothing that have been stored in the attic or the basement, or if they have been in a closet but not used for a long time. This applies even if the clothes have been stored in a closed cedar chest.
- Especially if you keep your shoes in a mudroom or garage, shake them out before putting them on.
- Clear away old furniture, tires, and other junk from yard areas. This will not greatly influence black widow populations, but will help reduce habitat for this spider (and improve the neighborhood!)
- Black widows prefer closed, dark places such as water meter compartments and crawl spaces, so construct barriers to inhibit entrance to these areas. Screen openings and plug holes and crevices with steel wool or other material.

114

☞ Most spiders have little defense against insecticides, and black widows are no exception. Apply an insecticide to the habitats frequented by these spiders when you detect an infestation. For the common black widow, spot treat directly on the web where the spider is found or suspected. Since the vast majority of spiders and other arthropods are either harmless or beneficial, treat only if you have an infestation or if you find one inside your home.

Symptoms of a Black Widow's Bite

The bold spider experimenter Mr. Baerg (see "Inquring Minds" on page 116) experienced many classic symptoms of a black widow bite, but, as with most victims, he did not die. Note, too, that it was not easy to induce the spider to attack. The effects of a black widow's bite are systemic, that is, felt throughout the body, and the symptoms below make respect for the spider easily understood:

☞ Initial pain similar to a pinprick at the bite that changes to a numbing pain of the affected area	☞ Numbness and tingling of the palms of the hands and bottoms of the feet
☞ Pregnant women may develop uterine contractions and premature labor	☞ Skin temperature over bite is warmer than surrounding area
☞ Muscle rigidity in the shoulders, back, chest	☞ Muscle cramps, particularly of the abdomen and back
☞ Chest muscle spasms and/or respiratory difficulty	☞ Children may cry persistently
☞ Nausea and/or vomiting	☞ Men may develop an erection
☞ Swelling or drooping eyelids	☞ Pain in the lymph nodes
☞ Increased perspiration	☞ Muscle pain
☞ Increased salivation	☞ Muscle twitching
☞ Facial swelling	☞ Skin rash or itching
☞ Restlessness	☞ Headache
☞ Anxiety	☞ Dizziness
☞ Drooling	☞ Fever
☞ High blood pressure	

{ insects & arachnids }

The characteristic cramping abdominal pain may be associated with pain in the flanks, thighs, or chest and be confused with acute appendicitis, renal stones, or acute myocardial infarction.

Will I Immediately Know I Have Been Bitten?

Maybe or maybe not. The puncture may just feel like a pinprick, but two tiny red spots may help you confirm the fact of a bite. If you've only got one puncture mark, it's very likely an insect bite (versus the spidery arachnids), but to be safe you should still monitor for the symptoms above. The wound may also appear as a bluish-red spot, surrounded by a whitish area.

Treatment for a Black Widow Spider Bite

☛ Apply ice packs to the bite. Place ice (wrapped in a washcloth or other suitable covering) on the site of the bite for ten minutes and then off for ten minutes. Repeat this process. If the patient has circulatory problems, decrease the time to prevent possible damage to the skin.

☛ Immediately transport the victim to a medical facility.

Once the victim is in the hospital, the doctor will have a number of therapies to use:

☛ Intravenous muscle relaxant medicines for muscle spasms and/or antihypertensive drugs for elevated blood pressure.

☛ Pain medicine.

INQUIRING MINDS

It's only within the last 100 years or so that any spiders were considered venomous to people. Prior to that, it was thought impossible that such a small creature could have such a big impact on a human. Then, according to entomologist Paul Hillyard, the London Natural History Museum's "Spiderman," a stouthearted southerner took a bold step:

The American arachnologist W. J. Baerg, of Fayetteville, Arkansas, made a brave gesture to scientific inquiry when in 1922 he arranged for himself to be bitten by a black widow. He survived the bite but suffered considerably and reported later: "The first test proved very difficult and ended in failure; it is not always easy to make the black widow bite. The second test resulted in all I could wish. The spider dug into the third finger of the left hand and held on till I removed her about 5 or 6 seconds later. The pain at first was faint but very soon began to increase into a sharp piercing sensation. In less than one hour the pain had reached the shoulder and within two hours the chest was affected; the diaphragm seemed partially paralyzed, breathing and speech became spasmodic. After 5 hours the pain extended to the legs and after 9 hours I was taken to hospital. A severe nausea and excruciating pain not only kept me awake but kept me moving throughout the night." (Hillyard, 1994, p. 70.)

☞ An antivenin, called "antivenin (*Latrodectus mactans*)" or black widow spider antivenin, for the most severe cases. It is available only through a physician and should be administered, if necessary, as soon as possible after the bite occurs. It is administered by injection.

Dr. Paul Auerbach, author of *Wilderness Medicine,* recommends the following:

> If you will be unable to reach a hospital within a few hours, and the victim is suffering severe muscle spasms, you may administer an oral dose of diazepam (Valium), if you happen to be carrying it. The starting dose for an adult who does not regularly take the drug is 5 milligrams, which can be augmented in 2.5-milligram increments every 30 minutes up to a total dose of 10 milligrams, so long as the victim remains alert and is capable of normal, purposeful swallowing. The starting dose for a child age 2 to 5 years is 0.5 milligrams; for a child age 6 to 12 years the starting dose is 2 milligrams. Total dose for a child should not exceed 5 milligrams; never leave a sedated child unattended.

Small children must receive antivenin as soon as possible and be treated in a hospital. Evacuate if you are camping, especially if symptoms do not begin to subside after 24 hours or if the person bit is under the age of 16, of small body weight, or elderly.

Considerations Prior to Using the Antivenin

☞ Tell your doctor if you have ever had an allergic reaction to black widow spider antivenin, to horses, or to any products of horse origin. You should also tell your doctor if you are regularly exposed to horses. Black widow spider antivenin contains horse serum.

☞ Tell your doctor if you have any other allergies, such as allergies to preservatives.

☞ Tell your doctor if you are pregnant. Envenomation by the black widow spider may result in miscarriages if left untreated.

☞ Tell your doctor if you are breast-feeding. It is unknown if the antivenin passes into the breast milk. Most medicines do pass into breast milk in small amounts, but many of them may be used safely while breast-feeding.

☞ Tell your doctor if you are using any other prescription or nonprescription (over-the-counter/OTC) medicine.

{ insects & arachnids }

Possible Side Effects of the Black Widow Antivenin

Confer with your doctor immediately if any of the following occur:

☞ Difficulty in breathing or swallowing

☞ Hives

☞ Itching, especially of feet or hands

☞ Reddening of skin, especially around ears

☞ Swelling of eyes, face, or inside of nose

☞ Unusual tiredness or weakness, especially if it is sudden and/or severe

These side effects below may occur, but they usually do not need medical attention. Do check with your doctor, though, if any of the following side effects continue or are demanding:

☞ Feeling of discomfort	☞ Fever
☞ Inflammation of joints	☞ Muscle aches
☞ Rash	☞ Swollen lymph glands

There may also be other side effects, so consult with your doctor if you are concerned.

Likelihood of Death from a Black Widow Bite

Death in a normally healthy individual is very rare. Full recovery usually takes about a week. Untreated, most people recover without help over the course of eight hours to two days. However, very small children and elderly victims may suffer greatly.

The common thinking is that the venom of a black widow spider is 15 times more potent than that of a rattlesnake, but the tiny amount injected is so minute their bites are not as likely to be fatal—three or four times less fatal by some estimates.

Yellow Sac Spiders

There is some debate about the impact of these creamy-to-golden-yellow arachnids. Their bite is believed to be venomous to humans, but rarely produces more than local symptoms. In fact, yellow sacs may produce a high percentage of the spider bites suffered by people. This is possibly so because they hunt at night when people cannot see well or are asleep, so the spiders may get accidentally squeezed and bite to protect themselves.

A large number of bites attributed to the brown recluse spider may actually be the result of yellow sac spider bites, which possess a cytotoxic venom. These enzymes can cause localized tissue necrosis (which may be similar to that caused by a recluse bite), though the symptoms are less severe and do not result in the systemic effects occasionally

Yellow Sac Spider (Cheiracanthium inclusum)

- The bite is generally mild and may or may not incur necrosis.
- It is common throughout most of the United States with the exceptions of northern New England and a curved pocket from western North Dakota to eastern Washington state down to Arizona and New Mexico.

YELLOW SAC SPIDER

- The body is 0.12 inch to .4 inch long. The leg span can be up to 1 inch long.
- The two common names (yellow sac and black-footed spider) derive from its appearance: pale yellow-beige color with dark brown markings on its palps (elongated appendages near the mouth), chelicerae (jaws), and on the ends of its tarsi (feet). There is also often an orange-brown stripe running down the top-center of its abdomen. The spider relies more on its palps than its eyes to sense its environment.
- Generally, during June and July females lay their eggs in small (.8 inch) silk tubes and enclose themselves with the eggs, protecting them from predators. They do not build webs.
- One of the most commonly encountered spiders in gardens. It hides under rocks and bark during the day, and wanders to the end of twigs and branches at night in search of roosting flies. In late summer and early fall, yellow sac spiders may migrate into buildings or automobiles, where they weave protective, silken, cocoon-like webs in which to pass the winter. These are immature spiders that will molt once more before reaching adulthood in the spring.
- This spider is nonaggressive and will bite under threat or attack, such as being squeezed in clothing. It is active at night.

{ insects & arachnids }

seen with recluse envenomations. Consequently, the view that this spider is dangerous to humans is questioned. A study of 20 confirmed yellow sac spider bites revealed no evidence of necrosis, and additional review of international literature on confirmed bites revealed only a single bite with mild necrotic symptoms.

Typical symptoms of a bite include an immediate stinging sensation followed by redness and mild swelling. Sometimes a blister may form at the site of the bite, often breaking, leaving a sore that heals over a period of several weeks. This spider's jaws cannot pierce the skin of everyone and may not inject venom on every bite, so there is a wide margin of safety.

Yellow sac spiders tend to be transported easily, particularly in agricultural products. Thus, they are widely distributed.

TICKS

If you live almost anywhere except inside a shopping mall or the equivalent, there's a host of ticks lurking and looking to hitch a ride on you to their next stage of life. These quiet, sneaky bloodsuckers top the "worst critter on earth" list of many people, and with good reason. At least with mosquitoes, which also bear serious diseases, you can see and hear them coming, but with ticks you look down and there they are—already crawling on you or dug in, dragging in their wake prolonged itching at best and disease at worst.

There are soft body ticks and hard body ticks, and although you might think that a "soft body" (filled with your blood) is the one to worry about, don't. They are not usually carriers of disease and are more prone to attack birds and mammals that have regular resting places. Of the hard body type, there are three species to be concerned about because of the diseases they carry.

Ticks to Track in the Chicago Area

The deer tick, also known as the black-legged tick (*Ixodes scapularis*), was at one time considered to be two species, but is now understood as one species that is distributed across the mid-western and eastern United States. In the northern reaches, populations at all stages feed on humans and animals. The deer tick is the primary vector for Lyme disease (*Borrelia burgdorferi*) and human granulocytic ehrlichiosis (HGE).

The wood tick, also known as the dog tick (*Dermacentor variabilis*), will feed on humans and domestic animals only in its adult stage. Immature stages typically feed on small rodents. This species can transmit Rocky Mountain spotted fever (*Rickettsia rickettsi* or RMSF) and is found in North America east of the Rocky Mountains and also in some western states such as California. The good news is that only 3–5 percent of adult ticks in RMSF areas carry the organism.

The lone star tick (*Amblyomma americanum*) is so named after the dramatic white spot on the female's back. This spot is actually iridescent, and so it can appear different colors depending on the light. All stages of this tick will feed on humans and domestic animals. Their larvae are known as "seed ticks"—they're that tiny—and are encountered in masses on vegetation, potentially resulting in hundreds of individual bites on one person. The good news is that if these little suckers don't get a blood meal, they will die after a killing frost in the fall. This species is known to transmit human monocytic ehrlichiosis (HME) (*Ehrlichia chaffeensis*).

It's more important to be familiar with the symptoms of the diseases than the species that bit you. The important things to do are:

☛ Remove ticks as soon as possible, which means checking twice a day or more if you are outside in areas where they are likely to be looking for a host.

☛ Watch for symptoms of the diseases ticks carry and seek medical attention right away if you think you have contracted a tick-borne illness.

☛ If you find yourself at the doctor's office with some of the symptoms listed below, tell your doctor if you've been bitten by or exposed to ticks lately. The faster you are correctly diagnosed for tick-borne illnesses, the better your chances of full recovery. Time is of the essence.

Parasitic Life Cycle

Ticks typically have four life stages—egg, larva, nymph, and adult. Except for the egg stage, each phase must have a separate animal host to complete its development, which may span two to three years. Blood-swelled mature females leave their hosts and lay a single mass of 3,000 to 6,000 eggs. These hatch into larvae that are just 0.025 of an inch in length. Right after hatching, these starving-for-blood larvae climb onto the nearest vegetation and wait for a warm-blooded animal to pass by. After grasping the feathers or hair of the unsuspecting beast, the young ticks insert their mouthparts and hook into the skin. After a two-to-three-day blood feast, the tick larvae drop off their host and begin to molt into nymphs. Ticks at this stage of life may survive the winter (hence, a problem with relatively mild winters), but at first blush of spring, they must feed again as soon as possible. After they do, they dismount their host again and molt into adults that likely will over-winter again before they emerge, hungry as ever in the spring and with a need

{ insects & arachnids }

Deer Tick (Ixodes scapularis)

- This tick is potentially lethal as a carrier for human granulocytic ehrlichiosis (HGE) and Lyme disease.
- It is found across the mid-western and eastern U.S as far north as Maine.
- Unengorged, it is 0.1 inch in length; gorged, 0.2 inch.
- Deer ticks are dark brown to black and often have black legs.
- The deer tick is found in wooded or grassy areas.
- Also known as the black-legged tick, this creature was at one time considered to be two species, but it is now understood as one. The distribution of *I. scapularis* is linked to the distribution and abundance of its primary reproductive host, white-tailed deer. Only deer or some other large mammal appears capable of supporting high populations of ticks.

DEER TICK AFTER SUPPER

not only to eat but also to mate. They feed on the next host, and then the cycle is set to repeat now that the female is ready to lay eggs again.

How They Feed

Ticks cut an entrance into a host's skin and insert their mouthparts. This feeding tube, the hypostome, has several rows of curved barbs that serve to anchor the tick to its host. This is why tick removal must be executed with gentle, steady care so as not to detach the tick head from the body. Blood is then pumped up by a muscular pharynx, and special glands secrete an anticoagulant in order to prevent the host's blood from clotting during the lengthy feeding period.

SPECIAL CONSIDERATIONS ABOUT DEER TICKS

Because deer ticks transmit Lyme disease, here a few extra facts:
- Deer ticks are most active from April through October.
- Deer ticks are hard to see. Nymphs are dot-sized and adults can be smaller than a sesame seed.
- If you discover a tick do not panic. The evidence suggests that an infected tick does not usually transmit the Lyme organism during the first 24 hours.

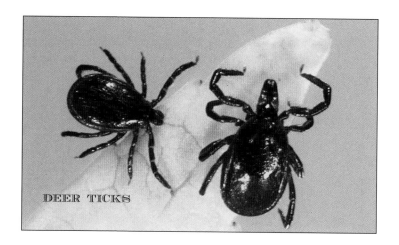

DEER TICKS

Tick Removal

☞ Grasp the tick just behind the point of attachment with a fine-point tweezers and pull straight out using slow, steady pressure until the tick is dislodged.

☞ Do not twist the tick as you remove it.

☞ Wash the bite area and apply an antiseptic.

☞ Do not use the unsafe, antiquated methods of applying gasoline, mineral oil, alcohol, kerosene, camp stove fuel, Vaseline, fingernail polish remover, or a match, a recently extinguished match head, or other hot object to the tick prior to removal. These practices are likely to make the tick struggle and vomit infectious fluids into the bite site. (Tick barf!)

☞ For deeply embedded ticks, apply the insecticide permethrin (such as Permanone), swabbing both the upper and lower sides of the tick with cloth or tissue. After 10 to 15 minutes, you should be able to pull the tick free. Carefully check the bite site for remaining head parts, and gently scrape them away using a sharp edge, such as a knife blade.

☞ If you use your fingers, grasp the tick using tissue paper or cloth. Children, elderly persons, and immuno-compromised persons may be at greater risk of infection and should especially use this procedure because infectious diseases carried by tick-fluid agents may enter through mucous membranes or breaks in the skin. This is the same reason not to crush ticks with your fingers.

☞ Nymphs, which are also known as "seed ticks," are sometimes present in such numbers that the United States Forest Service recommends removal by ripping them off your skin with a strip of duct tape before they can effectively burrow in.

{ insects & arachnids }

123

Tick Disposal

I have a friend who has such a war with ticks she used to keep a trophy jar filled with alcohol on her kitchen counter so she could readily see and show off to visitors how many of those "little bastards" she had pulled off herself and her dogs, some of which were quite large from engorging. In a junior-high-science-sort-of-way it was fascinating, but it didn't do much for the appetite. Still, her methodology was correct.

- ☞ Dropping them in alcohol is the surest, safest way to kill them.
- ☞ You can flush them down the toilet, but flush them right away. They will crawl out if you don't. We're not sure if they survive the trip through the sewage treatment plant (they're probably mutating for a revival X-Files episode as you read this), but I can't live with a jar of them. It's just a personal preference. Another friend sends them down her kitchen drain to save water.
- ☞ Burn them *after* you've removed them from your body.
- ☞ Don't try to mash them with your fingers. First, it's disgusting. Second, it's hard to do, especially if they are small. Third and most importantly, there is a slim chance that if they are carrying infection, it may enter your body if you have a small cut on your finger.
- ☞ If a single tick bite is a rare event for you, you may want to save the tick in a jar should you later develop disease symptoms. Preserve the tick by either adding some alcohol to the jar or by keeping it in the freezer. Identification of the tick may facilitate the physician's diagnosis and treatment. For those who find multiple ticks on them in any given season, however, this archival method is of less value in diagnosis.

When and Where They Are

- ☞ Ticks are present from early spring, as early as March in warmer areas, and they remain active until after the first freeze.
- ☞ Ticks love high grasses and brushy areas that provide shade and moisture. They hold on to a blade of grass with back legs, which leaves their forelegs available to grab a hold on anything passing by. Ticks can also be found in trees, and they can drop down on you.
- ☞ Ticks are common near stables, kennels, barns, or any other areas in which animals are kept.

Repelling and Discouraging Ticks

When in a tick-infested area, a good prevention is an insect repellent; however, consider using a product designed to be applied to clothing (permethrin products) rather than your skin. Although DEET is an

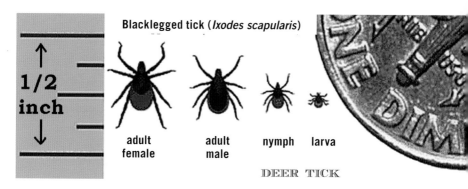

Blacklegged tick (*Ixodes scapularis*)

adult female   adult male   nymph   larva

DEER TICK

excellent mosquito repellant, it does not discourage ticks. Insecticides that contain permethrin can reduce tick infestations by 90 percent. Permanone is 0.5 percent permethrin. This is a spray application for clothing and is reported to be an excellent tick repellent.

- ☞ Tuck pants cuffs into boots or socks and wear long sleeves and light-colored clothing, which makes it easier to spot ticks. Some experts recommend putting tape around the area where pants and socks meet for added protection. Some people wrap small tick-prevention dog collars around their ankles *on the outside* of the pants tucked into socks.

- ☞ Stay to the center of hiking paths and avoid grassy and marshy woodland areas.

- ☞ Inspect yourself and your children for clinging ticks after leaving an infested area several times a day if the situation warrants it. Pay special attention to the hairy parts of the body and where clothing is snug against it. The sooner you remove a tick, the less chance it has to start spreading infections. When you get home, definitely inspect yourself carefully. Use a mirror to check difficult-to-observe parts of your body.

- ☞ If you suspect ticks in your clothing, wash them as soon as possible and use your dryer on a high heat setting.

- ☞ Ticks cannot easily tolerate direct sunshine, so keeping your grass cut short is one means of discouraging them in your yard. It also discourages rodents (a common host) from nesting. At its critical life stages, a tick must have a blood meal or die, so anything you can do to break that life cycle is a worthwhile endeavor.

- ☞ Sealing cracks and crevices inside your home and out can reduce entry points and hiding places.

- ☞ Dogs and cats are common carriers of ticks, but fortunately there are excellent products available from your veterinarian that, when used regularly, can virtually eliminate these parasites from your pets and ultimately from you. Some products are geared more toward tick

{ insects & arachnids }

prevention than others, so be sure to talk to your vet about all the options. Your animals will thank you, and you won't have to resort to "bombing" the inside of your house every summer, a practice with its own problems, risks, and inconveniences.

☞ In some cases creating a barrier around your yard by removing leaves and laying down a path of wood chips (2 to 4 feet wide) has reduced tick populations by between 44 to 88 percent.

☞ Guinea fowl (also known as "ginnies" and "peeps") will eat ticks, so if you want a flock, check your local civic ordinances and then go for it. They also make excellent "watch dogs" as they will raise a ruckus when strangers approach your yard.

☞ Call the Cook County agricultural extension agents at (773) 768-7779 if you have more ticks than you think you can take. They can recommend infestation treatments best suited to your area and needs.

Diseases Ticks Carry

It seems that nobody champions ticks. As one scientist said, "We are trying to come up with new ways to kill these little suckers as fast as we can. They are on mankind's hit list, not on the endangered species list."

A major reason to minimize the world's tick population is the diseases they spread. Although your chances of contracting a tick-borne disease are extremely small, do not underestimate the power and prevalence of these tiny, insidious creatures. Illinois tick-borne diseases are Rocky Mountain spotted fever (RMSF—very similar to tick fever), ehrlichiosis-tularemia, and Lyme disease. All are rare in the state.

PROS AND CONS OF DEET VERSUS PERMETHRIN:

• **DEET** needs to be applied regularly and can only work as it is evaporating. Permethrin works for weeks after it has dried inside clothing fibers.

• **DEET** is applied directly to the skin and can be absorbed through the skin. Permethrin is applied to clothing only and has limited contact to the skin.

• **DEET** has a detectable odor. Permethrin smells only until it dries.

• **DEET** does not kill or disable ticks and is a poor repellent. Permethrin works instantly and is extremely effective. It is the tick repellent of choice by the military.

• **DEET** can melt synthetic clothes like nylon. Permethrin causes no damage to any known cloth or synthetic fiber.

• **DEET** products are easy to find. Permethrin is hard to find and more expensive.

• **DEET** is an effective fish repellent, so anglers keep the DEET out of your tackle box. Permethrin's effect on fish is unknown.

• Permethrin-containing products that are approved for human use are manufactured by Coulston labs and can be found under labels such as Duranon, Permanone, and Congo Creek Tick Spray.

Rocky Mountain Spotted Fever

Rocky Mountain spotted fever (RMSF) is the most severe tick-borne rickettsial illness in the United States. This disease is caused by infection from the bacterial organism *Rickettsia rickettsii* that is transmitted through the bite of an infected tick. In Illinois the American dog tick *(Dermacentor variabilis)* is the primary vector of Rocky Mountain spotted fever bacteria. The incidence of infection in Illinois in 2008 was 1.5–19 cases per million population, according to the latest available CDC statistics. Rocky Mountain spotted fever can be contracted year-round, but May, June, and July are the peak months.

Rocky Mountain spotted fever was first recognized in 1896 in the Snake River Valley of Idaho and was originally called "black measles" because of the characteristic rash. It was a dreaded and frequently fatal disease that affected hundreds of people in that area. Rocky Mountain spotted fever remains a serious and potentially life-threatening infectious disease today, but fatalities are rare thanks to effective antibiotics. In the late 1940s, as many as 30 percent of persons infected with *R. rickettsii* died.

Symptoms of Rocky Mountain Spotted Fever

The first symptoms of Rocky Mountain spotted fever typically begin 2–14 days after the bite of an infected tick. A tick bite is usually painless and about half of the people who develop RMSF do not remember being bitten. The disease frequently begins as a sudden onset of fever and headache and most people visit a health-care provider during the first few days of symptoms. Because early symptoms may be nonspecific, several visits may occur before the diagnosis of RMSF is made and correct treatment begins. The following is a list of symptoms commonly seen with this disease; however, it is important to note that few people with the disease will develop all symptoms, and the number and combination of symptoms varies greatly from person to person.

- Fever
- Headache
- Nausea
- Vomiting
- Muscle pain
- Lack of appetite
- Conjunctival injection (red eyes)
- Abdominal pain (may mimic appendicitis or other causes of acute abdominal pain).
- Rash (occurs 2–5 days after fever, and may be absent in some cases).

Wood Tick (Dermacentor variabilis)

- The wood tick is potentially lethal as a carrier for Rocky Mountain spotted fever and tick fever.
- It is found in North America east of the Rocky Mountains and also in some western states such as California.
- Unengorged, it's 0.2 inch; gorged, 0.6 inch.
- The body is oval and flattened. Color is brown with whitish to grayish markings often with silvery hue.
- They are numerous along roads, paths, and trails, especially in grasses.
- Between the larvae, nymphs, and adults, the wood tick or "dog tick," as it is also known, is active from late March until about mid-September.

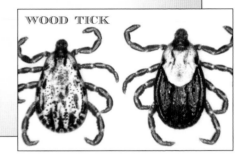

WOOD TICK

RMSF is a serious illness that can be fatal in the first eight days of symptoms if not treated correctly, even in previously healthy people. The progression of the disease varies greatly. Patients who are treated early may recover quickly on outpatient medication, while those who experience a more severe course may require intravenous antibiotics, prolonged hospitalization, or intensive care.

Rocky Mountain Spotted Fever Treatment

Doxycycline is the first-line treatment for adults and children of all ages and should be initiated immediately whenever RMSF is suspected. Use of antibiotics other than doxycycline is associated with a higher risk of fatal outcome. Treatment is most effective at preventing death if doxycycline is started in the first five days of symptoms. Therefore, treatment must be based on clinical suspicion alone and should always begin before laboratory results return or symptoms of severe disease, such as petechiae, develop.

If the patient is treated within the first five days of the disease, fever generally subsides within 24–72 hours. In fact, failure to respond to doxycycline suggests that the patient's condition might not be RMSF.

Rocky Mountain Spotted Fever's Potential Aftereffects

Treated in a timely manner with antibiotics for a standard five to ten days, RMSF can be cured with no long-term health problems. However, if not properly treated, an acute Rocky Mountain spotted fever infection can leave the following in its wake:

- ☛ Partial paralysis of the lower extremities.
- ☛ Gangrene requiring amputation of fingers, toes, arms, or legs.
- ☛ Hearing loss.
- ☛ Loss of bowel or bladder control.
- ☛ Movement disorders.
- ☛ Language disorders.

These complications are most frequent in persons recovering from severe, life-threatening cases, often following lengthy hospitalizations.

Ehrlichiosis

Ehrlichiosis is a tick-borne illness that is caused by an extremely small type of bacteria known as "ehrlichiae" that invade and live within white blood cells. These diseases are closely related to rickettsiae, the type of bacteria that cause Rocky Mountain spotted fever (RMSF). As with RMSF, your chances of contraction in Illinois are very slim (1.7–14 cases per million in 2008).

{ insects & arachnids }

129

Ehrlichiosis was first recognized as a disease in the United States in the late 1980s, but did not become a reportable disease until 1999. CDC compiles the number of cases reported by state health departments. Both *Ehrlichia chaffeensis* and *E. ewingii* are causes of human illness in the United States, although the majority of reported cases are due to *E. chaffeensis.*

The number of ehrlichiosis cases due to *E. chaffeensis* that have been reported to CDC has increased steadily since the disease became reportable, from 200 cases in 2000 to 961 cases in 2008. The incidence (the number of cases for every million persons) of ehrlichiosis increased similarly, from less than 1 case per million persons in 2000 to 3.4 cases per million persons in 2008. During the same time period, the annual case fatality rate (the proportion of ehrlichiosis patients that died as a result of their infections) has declined.

Symptoms of Ehrlichiosis

Symptoms begin in 1 to 21 days following infection (the average is 7 days), and they resemble those of Rocky Mountain spotted fever. They vary greatly in severity, ranging from an illness so mild that no medical attention is sought, to a severe, life-threatening condition. The most common symptoms are:

- High fever
- Headache
- Chills
- Muscular aches and pains

But may also include:

- Nausea
- Vomiting
- Loss of appetite
- An overall feeling of bodily discomfort

Rash is rare, but when present it may resemble the spotted rash of RMSF, although it is usually less prominent and more variable in appearance and location. Since ehrlichiae invade white blood cells, the body's immune system is compromised. That lessens the body's ability to fight other infections so complications can quickly arise, and in the most severe cases kidney or respiratory failure occurs. There have been a number of deaths associated with both HME and HGE.

Treatment for Ehrlichiosis

Blood tests can confirm the diagnosis. The antibiotic doxycycline is very effective and when used early the disease can be completely defeated. However, because ehrlichiosis can be so severe, or even deadly, it is very important to obtain early diagnosis and treatment, as it is with all the tick-borne illnesses.

Tularemia

In Illinois the dog tick (*Dermacentor variabilis*) and the lone star tick (*Amblyomma americanum*) are also carriers of tularemia, which is also carried by rabbits. From 2001–2010 two cases were reported in the Chicago area. For more information on this disease please see the entry in the mammals section on page 47.

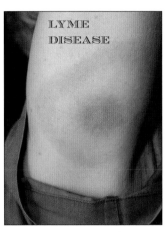

Lyme Disease

The most commonly reported vector-borne disease, Lyme disease is caused by infection with the spirochete *Borrelia burgdorferi*, transmitted to humans by infected deer ticks (*Ixodes scapularis*) and black-legged ticks (*I. pacificus ticks*). Lyme disease bacteria are maintained in the blood systems of small rodents and are not transmitted from person to person. For example, you cannot get infected from touching or kissing a person who has Lyme disease, or from a health-care worker who has treated someone with the disease. Having had Lyme disease doesn't protect against reinfection.

Where Is Lyme Disease Concentrated in the United States?

In 2010, 94 percent of Lyme disease cases were reported from 12 states:

- Connecticut
- Delaware
- Maine
- Maryland
- Massachusetts
- Minnesota
- New Jersey
- New Hampshire
- New York
- Pennsylvania
- Virginia
- Wisconsin

From 2005–2010 there has been a national annual average of approximately 26,600 cases. Looking at 2000–2010 in Illinois, the incidence rate is 1.1 per 100,000 people. Lyme disease is rarely, if ever, fatal.

More Information

Due to the low incidence of these tick-born diseases, please direct your curiosity to the Centers for Disease Control and Prevention's excellent website at cdc.gov. This site has provided substantial data for this chapter and other parts of this volume.

{ insects & arachnids }

MITES

Mites are minute arachnids, ranging from near invisibility to more than an inch long. Most usually measure 0.125 inch or less in length. Together with their buddies the ticks, which also share the Acarina order, these creatures comprise more than 30,000 known species worldwide, and the National Audubon Society estimates there are probably at least 1 million species yet to be identified. Mites' bodies resemble those of ticks—oval, elongated, and unseparated into cephalothorax and abdomen.

Many mites are beneficial, preying on aphid eggs, for example, or chowing down on other insects. But there are a couple of mites worthy of examination here. Both are parasitic at some point during their four-stage life cycle (egg, larva, nymph, adult), and, more importantly, both can make you itch enough to think you are going to lose your mind. I am speaking, of course, of chiggers and scabies.

Chiggers

> *"I'm hosting a party Friday night."*
>
> > *"Really. Well, I'm hosting a chigger colony."*

From "In Defense of Mosquitoes," a story by Vicki Edwards

The word chigger reportedly comes from the Wolof (African) word "jiga," and Caribbean islanders call tropical sand fleas "chigoes," probably a linguistic mutation from the same African origin. They also go by the name of red bugs because they are, in fact, orange-red in color, if only you could see them with your naked eyes, which you usually don't—and that's part of the problem. They cling to you, do their dirty work, and split probably before you even know they paid you a visit. Chiggers (*Sarcoptes scabiei var. hominis*) resemble tiny, tiny ticks, and it's a rare person who has not experienced their invidious itch. They don't do any-thing more serious, however, than drive you crazy.

CHIGGER

Chiggers are so well known that internationally respected artist Red Grooms immortalized them with a caricature on his "Fox Trot Carousel" located in downtown Nashville. The chigger ride on this working carousel is an anatomical digression from the real thing, but Red has captured the mean-spirited heart of the beast. His chigger looks like a bloated science-fiction-sized mosquito on LSD, with bloodshot eyes, a long probing snout, and a definite "Yeah? So what're you gonna do about it?" attitude.

Chiggers are the larvae of the harvest mite, those creatures that look like small, velvety red spiders you see on the soil surface when turning the garden soil during the warm days of springtime. Around this time of year, these adults lay eggs in the soil that hatch into the larval chigger.

Although the harvest mite adults and most immature stages are completely harmless, the larval stage is a parasite on many animals: rodents, birds, poultry, rabbits, livestock, snakes, and toads, as well as humans. Chiggers move very quickly on the ground and they can rapidly crawl onto your feet or legs. On board the necessary host for the protein meal for its next stage of life, the chigger usually moves about until it reaches a place where it is somewhat confined. Vexing locales such as around ankles, under socks, behind knees, in the groin or armpit, and anywhere that elastic meets skin are desirable. Chiggers can wander for hours on a host, selecting just the right real estate before settling down to feed.

In about 3 to 24 hours after initial feeding by the chigger, and depending on the reaction of the host, a characteristic red, intense, itching welt appears on the skin. If removed before completion of feeding, larval chiggers will not bite again and eventually die. The longer a chigger is attached, the larger the welt and the greater the itching.

Contrary to popular belief, chiggers do not burrow into the skin, but do pierce it (often around a hair follicle), to inject a fluid that prevents blood from clotting and causes a red welt with a white, hard central area. The tiny, red chigger in the center of the itching bump is effectively camouflaged by the inflamed tissues. When our bodies produce histamines to combat this anticoagulant fluid, the itching begins. After a belly full and a beer (just kidding), the chigger drops from its host and goes into the ground for an inactive stage. In the fall it becomes a bright red adult with four pairs of legs and spends its winter in the ground.

Are There Chiggers There?

To check out whether an area is infested with chiggers, place six-inch squares of black paper vertically in the grass. These will become covered with chiggers that will look like tiny yellow or pink dots moving around if chiggers are present. They are found in clumps, which is why they can overwhelm you, and your party mate may be left unscathed. They become less active at temperatures below 60 degrees Fahrenheit.

Chigger Country

Chiggers are basically "bags of water," therefore needing high humidity to keep from drying out and dying. They are most likely to be found in areas where vegetation is thick and where there is an abundance of moisture and shade:

- ☞ At the woodland borders.
- ☞ Along the periphery of swamps.
- ☞ In shrub thickets.
- ☞ In unmowed areas of lawn.
- ☞ In thick layers of pine straw, leaf litter, or thatch.

Treatment of Chigger Bites

- ☞ Don't wait for the red welt or the itch. Chiggers are easily dislodged by gentle rubbing, even if attached. If you have been in "chigger country," bathing immediately after exposure and lathering your entire body with soap several times and scrubbing with a washcloth may reduce the number of bites. If you cannot bathe immediately after walking in a chigger-infested area, rubbing yourself down with a towel or cloth may be of benefit.
- ☞ Wash your clothes to prevent reinfection. To the extent that chiggers are like ticks, they may require a high-heat dryer cycle to kill them.
- ☞ To relieve itching, over-the-counter lotions and ointments containing antihistamine and/or hydrocortisone formulated with an anti-itch remedy such as lidocaine or benzocaine may be helpful. "Painting" bites with clear nail polish to destroy the chigger is probably not effective because by the time the bite itches, the chigger is probably no longer there, and you don't want to hold on to that sucker anyway, do you?

PREVENTION OF CHIGGER BITES

- Chiggers are attracted to their host by carbon dioxide, so stop breathing. (Hello?)
- Eliminate shade to help reduce the number of chiggers in an area.
- Keep your lawn trimmed to prevent favorable breeding sites and reduce populations.
- Keep outdoor walkways tidy.
- Eliminate tall weeds and shrubs—particularly berry patches that furnish food for rodent and bird hosts of mites.
- Chiggers don't like DEET, so you can apply those types of repellents to shoes, socks, pants cuffs, ankles and legs, and around your waist (on the outside of your clothes only).

Chigger (*Trombicula larvae*)

- Chiggers cause intense itching.
- They are found along the Atlantic coast through the Mid-West and into the southwestern United States.
- They grow to 0.01 inch.
- They are six-legged as larvae and colored red to pale yellow or white and eight-legged and red as adults.
- They are common in fields, especially during the autumn.
- Chiggers are most abundant in areas that support thickets or scrub-type vegetation and where the ground is undisturbed, supporting many rabbits, other rodents, and various small host animals. They are generally eliminated automatically by habitat destruction in areas that are heavily populated or intensively farmed. In new urban subdivisions, however, chiggers may persist in lawns for several years.

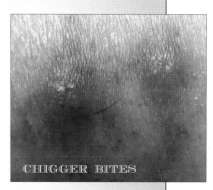
CHIGGER BITES

☞ Oral antihistamines may help, too.

☞ Repeated scratching of the welt may cause additional wounding of the skin and result in secondary infection, so try not to scratch (right!) and keep the welt area clean.

☞ If a severe reaction develops consult your physician.

Other (untested by the author) remedies include:

☞ A home remedy using meat tenderizer (papain without salt), or baking soda, fashioned into a paste and rubbed onto the welt has been known to reduce itching.

☞ Sponging vinegar or a diluted solution of bleach (1 part bleach: 10 parts water) on welts has also been reported, by some, to help reduce itching.

Scabies

Scabies is an infestation of the skin with the microscopic mite *Sarcoptes scabei*. Infestation is common, found worldwide, and affects people of all

{ insects & arachnids }

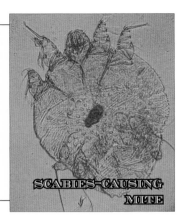

Scabies- Causing Mite (Sarcoptes scabiei)

- They cause intense itching.
- They are found worldwide.
- They may grow to the size of a pinhead.
- They live on the human body.
- You don't want them.

SCABIES-CAUSING MITE

races and social classes. Scabies spreads rapidly under crowded conditions where there is frequent skin-to-skin contact between people, such as in hospitals, institutions, childcare facilities, and nursing homes.

This mite is about the size of a pinhead and can live only two to three days at room temperature apart from the human body. It burrows into the outer layer of skin and lays eggs that hatch in three to five days. After hatching, the newly formed mites leave the burrow and move to other skin surfaces and repeat the cycle.

More Than a Handshake

Scabies is spread by direct skin-to-skin contact with a person already infested with scabies. Contact must be prolonged (a quick handshake or hug will usually not spread infestation), but infestation is easily spread to sexual partners and household members. Infestation may also occur by sharing clothing, towels, and bedding. People with weakened immune systems and the elderly are at risk for a more severe form of scabies, called Norwegian or crusted scabies.

Once away from the human body, mites do not survive more than 48 to 72 hours. When living on a person, an adult female mite can live up to a month.

Diagnosis is most commonly made by looking at the burrows or rash. A skin scraping may be taken to look for mites, eggs, or mite fecal matter to confirm the diagnosis. Typically, there are fewer than ten mites on the entire body of an infested person; this makes it easy for an infestation to be missed.

Symptoms of Scabies

☞ For a person who has never been infested with scabies, symptoms may take four to six weeks to begin. For a person who has had scabies, symptoms appear within several days. There is no immunity to an infestation.

☞ Pimple-like irritations, burrows, or rash of the skin large enough to see with the naked eye, especially on the webbing between the fingers; the skin folds on the wrist, elbow, or knee; the penis, the breast, or shoulder blades. The burrows look like grayish-white lines or tracks that zigzag on the skin surface.

☞ Intense itching, especially at night and over most of the body.

☞ Sores on the body caused by scratching that can sometimes become infected with bacteria.

Can You Get Scabies from Your Pet?

The Centers for Disease Control says no. Pets have a different kind of scabies mite (also called mange). If your pet has mange and has close contact with you, the mite can get under your skin and cause itching and skin irritation. However, this type of mite dies in a couple of days and does not reproduce. You may itch for several days, but you do not need to be treated with special medication to kill the mites. Until your pet is successfully treated, though, mites can continue to burrow into your skin and cause you to have symptoms.

Treatment of Scabies

Anyone who is diagnosed with scabies, as well as his or her sexual partners and people who have close, prolonged contact to the infested person, should also be treated. If your health-care provider has instructed family members to be treated, everyone should receive treatment at the same time to prevent reinfestation.

Products used to kill scabies mites are called scabicides. Scabicides used to treat human scabies are available only with a doctor's prescription. No "over-the-counter" (nonprescription) products have been tested and approved to treat human scabies. Apply lotion to a clean body from the neck down to the toes and leave overnight (eight hours).

COCKROACHES

Perhaps you've heard the joke: At the end of the world there will still be cockroaches and Cher. In fact, cockroaches are among the hardiest insects on the planet. Some species are capable of remaining active for a month without food and are able to survive on limited resources like the glue from the back of postage stamps. Some can go without air for 45 minutes. In one experiment, cockroaches were able to recover from being submerged underwater for half an hour.

{ insects & arachnids }

American Cockroach (Periplaneta americana)

- Cockroaches can transmit diseases and bacteria, but their most annoying aspect is that they can trigger allergic reactions, particularly in people prone to asthma. You could get skin rashes, watery eyes, nasal congestion, and even asthma attacks.
- Due to commerce, the American cockroach is found throughout the world.
- They are generally 1.2 inches long at maturity.
- Cockroaches thrive in warm, humid conditions. They prefer to live in kitchens and other food-preparation areas, so they can feed off food spills and have plenty of water to drink.
- They like to hide in cracks in walls, confined spaces, in a pantry or underneath a stack of magazines, newspapers or cardboard boxes, kitchen cupboards, below sinks, around water heaters, and in drains and grease traps.
- Except for the Asian cockroach, all cockroaches are nocturnal, and of the three main species only the American cockroach can fly.

AMERICAN COCKROACH

It's part of popular culture that cockroaches will "inherit the earth" if humanity destroys itself in a nuclear war. In fact, cockroaches do have a much higher radiation resistance than vertebrates, with the lethal dose perhaps 6 to 15 times that for humans.

Cockroaches are one of the most commonly noted household pest insects. They feed on human and pet food, and can leave an offensive odor, a kind of sickly sweetness. They can also passively transport microbes on their body surfaces including those that are potentially dangerous to humans, particularly in environments such as hospitals. However, and paradoxically, they are fastidious animals that are comparable to cats in this regard.

Cockroaches have been linked to allergic reactions in humans, particularly asthma. They may also trigger nonfatal allergic reactions for people who respond poorly to exposure to shrimp, mollusks, or dust mites.

Discouraging Cockroaches

☞ Keep all food stored away in sealed containers.
☞ Use garbage cans with tight lids.
☞ Frequently clean the kitchen.
☞ Vacuum regularly.
☞ Repair any water leaks, such as dripping taps.
☞ Seal off any entry points, such as holes around baseboards, in between kitchen cabinets, pipes, doors, and windows with some steel wool or copper mesh and some cement, putty, or silicone caulk.

Getting Rid of Cockroaches

If you want to invite wasps or house centipedes (*Scutigera coleoptrata*) into your home, they will take care of your roach problem. If this solution fails to please you, there are many products and services on the market.

You can make an inexpensive roach trap with a deep smooth-walled jar. An inch or two of beer inside will attract the roaches. Help the roaches to enter the jar by placing the rim against a wall, or construct a ramp with sticks leading up to the top. Once inside, the roaches will not be able to climb back out and will drown. You can also smear a bit of Vaseline on the inside of the jar to enhance slipperiness. The method is sometimes called the "Vegas roach trap" after it was popularized by a Las Vegas-based TV station that used coffee grounds and water. Personally, I'd rather undergo death-by-beer, but that's your call.

{ insects & arachnids }

139

BLACK-AND-YELLOW
MUD DAUBER

HONEYBEE

SADDLEBACK CATERPILLAR

reptiles &
amphibians

It doesn't take long for a discussion about dangerous reptiles and amphibians to get around to snakes. In the Chicago area your chances of a venomous snake encounter are very slim. There is only the Massasauga rattlesnake. Unfortunately, this species is endangered—but not extinct—so in this chapter you have all you need to know about snakebites. It is important to remember that most of the snakes you will see are harmless and just want to be left alone. There's also the snapping turtle, which can bite off a finger, but, as usual, these critters would rather retreat than attack. If cornered, however, the snapping turtle can be a formidable foe. The common American toad is more of a danger to your pets than to you, but its skin secretions can cause problems for humans. It's always wise to be aware of and understand the wild creatures that reside where you live and recreate.

SNAKES

The sight of a snake strikes an emotional chord in most people quite out of proportion with the reptile's potential for causing harm. Statistically, you have a better probability of being killed by lightning. Unfortunately, ignorance is legion when it comes to snakes, and it's compounded by myth and misinformation. Most snake stories begin with a snake and end with a big rock or a shotgun. And, of course, the snake in every story was venomous and launching a direct frontal assault.

Most snakes are harmless, and many snakes, including North America's relatively few venomous species, feed on insects, rats, mice, and other vermin. In the woods and in the neighborhood, snakes are good neighbors, on patrol around the clock helping Orkin keep pests under control. Plus, when's the last time you were kept awake at night by a barking snake?

If you are an avid outdoors person, you might see a snake in the wild twice a year. If you are only an occasional visitor to the great outdoors, you might go an entire lifetime without encountering a snake. No matter where you live, harmless, nonvenomous species outnumber venomous species by a great margin, so the probability of stumbling onto a venomous snake is very remote. Most of the time, if you do chance upon a venomous snake, you will not be attacked or bitten unless you do something really, really stupid. Finally, even if you are bitten, there's about a 30 percent probability (depending on the species) that the snake will not inject venom. So, you see, there's really no reason to be neurotic about snakes. For self-confidence and peace of mind, however, it's helpful to know a thing or two about our down-to-earth friends.

How People Are Bitten by Snakes

It may amaze you to know that most snakebites, both venomous and nonvenomous, occur as a direct result of trying to handle snakes. Because, in this instance, the way to avoid being bitten is so obvious, I won't dwell on it.

Many harmless and most venomous snakes hunt at night. This means they hole up during the day in brush, stacked firewood, lumber piles, and the like, as well as in rock crevices, under rocks, and around streambeds. Bites to the hands, arms, feet, and legs occur when working outdoors clearing brush; moving debris, lumber, or firewood; or putting your hands into rock crevices or under rocks. Hiking off trail, especially in cane or tall grass, likewise increases the chances of stepping on or near a snake that you don't see.

Other frequently occurring situations leading to snakebite involve trying to kill, remove, or chase away a snake. If you find a snake in your yard, tapping it gently with a long pole or broom handle (while maintaining a safe distance) should suffice to move it along. Even if you positively identify the snake as venomous, you're less at risk by allowing it to move off on its own (or with a little persuasion from your broom) than you are trying to kill it. First, it wouldn't be around in the first place if there wasn't something to eat, and, second, assuming the snake occurs naturally in your neck of the woods, there will be more to take the place of the one you kill.

Doctors treat dozens of folks every year who injure themselves trying to kill snakes. Ricocheting pellets, BBs, and buckshot cause more eye injuries than you would believe, and people have also been known to club themselves (and others) with shovels and hack themselves (and others) with axes while flailing away at a snake. Sometimes less-than-cautious individuals capture a snake only to be bitten through the burlap bag or pillowcase they've tossed it in, and, incredibly, a number of people are even bitten by dead snakes (more on this later). It's a dangerous world out there. Make it a little saner by respecting snakes and giving them space.

Nonvenomous Snakes

Nonvenomous snakes are found virtually everywhere, from your backyard to the mountains to the swamp. If one bites you, you'll experience very little pain—but figuratively speaking, you'll spill enough adrenaline to set a world record in the high jump. When you calm down, you'll discover a horseshoe pattern of small needle-like pricks where you were chomped. Like any wild animal bite, infection is a possibility (you don't know who that snake's been kissing), so wash the wound well with soap and water and then apply a disinfectant.

If you watch A&E or the Discovery Channel on television, you've probably seen a show or two about big constricting snakes like boas, pythons, and anacondas that dine on just about anything from antelopes to puppies. Well, the good news is that (except as pets) those snakes don't live in Illinois.

Venomous or Nonvenomous?

First, there are only four kinds of venomous snakes that you have to worry about in the entire U.S.: the coral snake, the copperhead, the cottonmouth (also called the water moccasin), and the rattlesnake. The massasaga rattlesnake is the only venomous snake in the Chicago area.

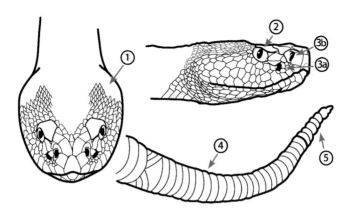

VENOMOUS SNAKES

☛ 1. Head distinctly triangular, when viewed from above.

☛ 2. Pupils elliptical.

☛ 3. Pits(a) as well as nostrils(b) present.

☛ 4. Undivided scales on underside of tail.

☛ 5. Except for the Northern copperhead, tail ends in a rattle.

The fact that it is an endangered species makes it all the less likely you will have an encounter. Just to satisfy your curiosity, however, I give you a general overview of U.S. snakes.

The coral snake is a member of the cobra family (Elapidae), while the other venomous snakes found in the U.S. are pit vipers (Crotalidae). Pit vipers, including rattlesnakes, copperheads, and cottonmouths, are so called because of an orifice or "pit" between the eyes and nostrils. Rich with nerve endings and covered by a membrane, the pit helps the snake sense the presence and whereabouts of warm-blooded prey or predators. The pit has been compared to a highly directional dish microphone that can pick up a quarterback's calls from the sidelines. It functions extremely well as a type of radar that enables the snake to "see" its prey or an aggressor solely by heat—not by light, sound, or touch. Elliptical pupils, a swollen-looking head, and undivided subcaudal (underneath the tail) scales are likewise identifying features of pit vipers.

It is important to note, however, according to the exceptional venomous snake expert Laurence M. Klauber, that some nonvenomous species also have some of these attributes, so it is unsafe to rely solely on this criteria. He maintains that the "only unfailing method is an examination

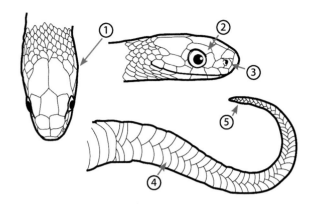

of the snake for hollow or grooved fangs and venom glands, and this will not disclose the degree of danger from its bite." (Klauber, 1997, p. 23) Perhaps you'll agree this is not a job for anyone other than a professional herpetologist. In light of this, your job is to learn as much as you can about truly dangerous snakes, and, chiefly, to give snakes their due—meaning a wide berth. Blind fear of all snakes, or even of venomous snakes, is not a good line of defense. Knowledge is.

A Harmless Snake's Defense

When threatened, many harmless snakes will put on an aggressive display. They may at times overcompensate in these theatrics, for unlike the venomous rattler, for example, they have no real lethal weapon to use. Bluffing behavior can include coiling, vibrating the tail (which in leaves can send your heart racing and should stop you in your tracks for assessment), hissing, and lunging. Klauber says it well with his characteristic dry humor: "But it is all bluff; and the difference between being struck by a gopher snake and a rattler is the difference between being hit by two falling objects—a feather in one case, a safe in the other." (Klauber, 1997, p. 22)

{ reptiles & amphibians }

147

"Mr. Fangman"

All venomous snakes have fangs, whereas nonvenomous snakes do not. Nonvenomous snakes have, however, lots of small sharp teeth that are quite capable of breaking the skin. A bite from a nonvenomous snake will look like a series of pinpricks arrayed in a horseshoe pattern. A bite from a venomous snake will leave puncture marks from the fangs. Usually there will be two fang marks, but even venomous snakes miss from time to time, so it's possible to be hit by only one of the fangs. Nonvenomous snakes in the U.S. have a habit of biting and holding on. People who keep nonvenomous species as pets sometimes have to pry the snake's jaws open following a bite in order to remove the snake.

All pit vipers (rattlers, copperheads, cottonmouths) in the U.S. usually strike and release. Sometimes some entanglement such as clothing will make release more difficult, but this is not the behavioral norm. Pit viper fangs rotate forward when striking and fold back against the roof of the mouth when not in use. Each rests in a sheath of soft membranous skin. The maxillary bones rotate the fangs forward when the need to strike arises. As in a fine machine, venom ducts transport venom from glands into the empty sheaths so that venom is forced into the top of each fang and is expelled out of the opening near the tip.

If you've got one or two fang marks, it's definitely time to hop in the car (get someone else to drive if possible) and make an advance call to the hospital to say that you're on your way.

Copperheads are small-to-medium-sized snakes with fangs long enough to pierce clothing and footwear. While not to be discounted, they are not as great a threat as are larger rattlers and cottonmouths, which can deliver huge amounts of venom through long fangs.

Nasty Babies

All venomous snakes are born fully equipped with venom and fangs. Often young snakes (harmless and otherwise) will be more pugnacious and ready to defend themselves, so it's wise not to discount a snake just because it's small.

Up from the Grave He Arose and Bit Poor Lucy on the Nose

Sometimes people are bitten while handling a dead pit viper. A curious postmortem muscle contraction in the snake can result in a bite to the handler. Although rare, such bites have been known to occur even when the head was maimed or severed from the body.

DISTRIBUTION OF U.S. SNAKEBITES ON THE BODY
(*Klauber*, 1997, p. 849)

Arm 9.94%	Total limbs 98.43%
Hand or wrist 12.92%	Trunk .69%
Finger 18.06%	Head .88%
Leg 22.07%	Head and Trunk 1.57%
Foot or ankle 35.44%	Upper limb 40.92%
Lower limb 57.51%	

Because most victims have ample opportunity to seek emergency treatment, there are very few fatalities from venomous snakebites. However, surviving the bite is no picnic either. Pit viper bites especially are quite painful and can cause a great deal of long-term tissue damage in the area of the bite. Long-term results can include: amputation, memory loss, difficulty with mental calculations, severe scarring, and pain.

Really Bad Spit

You may be surprised to learn that, like human saliva, the poison of venomous snakes consists mainly of enzymes. When we chew, our saliva initiates the digestive process by helping break down whatever we're eating. The same thing happens when a snake injects venom into its victim. The enzymes in the venom begin digesting the prey even before the victim is swallowed. Snake venom, of course, is more potent than our saliva and works on the snake's prey in ways that are quite different from the role our saliva plays in the human digestive process. Because most venomous snakes strike, inject venom, and release, the prey often runs some distance before it succumbs to the poison and dies. The snake uses its Jacobson's organ—a chemoreceptor situated within paired cavities in the roof of the mouth (as well as its pit if a pit viper)—that relays a combination of smell and taste to track and find the terminally wounded prey. A snake's famous forked tongue collects data for the Jacobson's organ by air sampling.

Understanding Venom: Attacking Blood or Nerves

Most snake venom is comprised of both hemorrhagic and neurotoxic elements, though overall there's a wide variety of venom components and mixtures. The hemorrhagic chemicals in snake venom destroy the lining and walls of the blood vessels, destroy red blood corpuscles, and prevent the coagulation of blood. The victim, in other words, bleeds to death from the inside. Neurotoxins in snake venom act on the bulbar and spinal ganglion cells of the central nervous system; they shut down the nervous system, resulting in cardiac arrest and the cessation of respiration. Although

{ reptiles & amphibians }

149

snake venom may include some hemorrhagic *and* neurotoxic elements, pit viper bites cause primarily hemorrhagic symptoms.

To assess the seriousness of a snakebite, you must consider the type of venom, the potency of the venom, the amount of venom injected, and the location of the bite on the body. Larger copperheads can inject a goodly amount of venom. Their predominantly hemorrhagic venom, however, works somewhat slowly and has decidedly less effect on the nervous system than other venomous snakes.

Most snakebites are inflicted below the knees or on the hands or forearms. Bites on the upper and lower extremities are less life threatening than bites closer to the heart.

Risk Assessment

If you are walking, hiking, or mountain biking on a marked trail, it's possible, though unlikely, you will encounter a snake. Your chances increase during the spring and fall when snakes make use of the trail's surface to warm themselves, and when the snakes are also more likely to be on the move. In the summer, snakes stay under cover most of the day but may stretch out on the trail in the late afternoon and evening to soak up the residual heat from the surface of the trail. Snakes might make use of a quiet road or driveway for the same purpose.

You are at greatest risk when you leave the trail or road and strike off through the woods. The pit vipers, especially, are masters of camouflage.

TIMING OF BITES

To no one's surprise, late spring into early fall is when most bites occur. Snakes are prone to hibernation, but you cannot absolutely rule out activity through the winter, since the following table indicates a full calendar of bites.

Monthly Distribution of Snakebites in the U.S. (*Klauber*, 1997, p. 853)

January: 7	February: 1	March: 23	April: 83
May: 116	June: 168	July: 252	August: 191
September: 158	October: 65	November: 19	December: 5

In the U.S., an average of 8 to 15 deaths per year occur as a result of snakebites, almost all from rattlesnake bites (lethal bites from nonindigenous species are also included in the data). Copperhead envenomation causes effects similar to rattlesnake envenomation, but is generally less serious. With these, the most common symptoms and signs are limited to local pain and swelling. The AAPCC has reported no deaths from copperhead envenomation since its first annual report in 1983. Overall in the U.S. and Canada, the risk of dying from a venomous snakebite is far less than being killed by lightning, wasps, or bees.

The harmless hog-nosed snake (above) with its fat body and triangular head is often confused with a rattlesnake.

Sometimes they look like a tree root or blend perfectly with dried grass, brush, or leaves. Off-trail, it's easy to step on or close to an unseen snake. If you are working outdoors, beware of brush piles, downed trees, refuse, woodpiles, and other cool, shady places that snakes occupy to avoid the heat.

You can minimize your risk by staying on a marked trail and keeping a watchful eye. The more open and clear the trail, the easier snakes are to spot. While on the trail, always be vigilant, especially at creek crossings, in rocky areas, and when stepping over fallen trees and branches. Make a habit of stepping onto rocks and logs, clearing the far side by a foot or more as you proceed.

Although all snakes can and do climb, venomous species in the U.S. are not considered arboreal. This means that you do not have to worry about a venomous snake dropping on you out of a tree while walking. If you are in a boat, it's possible (though highly unlikely) that a venomous snake could drop off of an eye-level (or lower) branch into your boat. The startled reptile's intention, of course, is to evade danger by slipping into the water. Speaking of water, venomous snakes in the U.S. can bite both in and under water.

In the U.S., approximately 7,000 to 8,000 reptile bites are reported annually to the American Association of Poison Control Centers (AAPCC). However, this figure is conservative due to under-reporting. Males are more commonly bitten than females, with young adults (in the age group 18 to 28 years) receiving 50 percent of all bites.

{ reptiles & amphibians }

Copperheads are responsible for about 24 percent of venomous snakebites nation wide. Dry bites, in which there is no envenomation, occur in as many as 50 percent of all venomous species strikes.

Avoidance and Precaution

When exploring the outdoors, always tell someone where you are going and when you expect to return. In areas where there are venomous snakes, walk, hike, camp, bike, or work accompanied by at least two companions when possible. If someone is bitten, one person can stay with the victim while the other goes for help. If there are fewer than three people, carry a cell phone. If you come across any snake in the field and don't know positively what it is (or isn't), do not approach it, try to examine it, or photograph it (unless you have a long telephoto or zoom lens). Carry the first-aid items discussed below and know how to use them.

Encounters

All snakes exhibit a wide range of alertness. A snake on the move will be fully alert, whereas one stretched sunning on a rock or trail may or may not be. A snake's eyes are open all of the time, even when it's sleeping, so you can't judge its wakefulness by observing the eyes. If the snake feels threatened it will flee or assume a defensive posture. This could be as unremarkable as redirecting its gaze to take you in, or as dramatic as coiling. Often, however, the snake will be quite lethargic. In this case it will probably not acknowledge your presence. Snakes sunning on a highway often have to be prodded so they won't become road-kill.

Because it takes some experience to gauge a snake's relative alertness, your best bet is to give it a wide berth. In specific terms, pass the snake at a distance at least equal to its body length. If the trail is too narrow to pass the snake at a safe distance, use a long stick to gently prod it off the trail and out of the way. The idea here is to move the snake along without unduly arousing it. Under no circumstances approach closer than one body length of the snake. If a long stick is not available, tossing small pebbles, sand, or twigs at the snake will usually make it move.

A snake may be sleeping during the day because it was active at night. With their food sources active at night, snakes are often prowling about in the dark, so (cautiously!) gather that firewood earlier in the day.

The Eternal Dilemma:
What to Wear in Venomous Snake Country?

☞ Boots, at least to knee height, will help considerably. These should be constructed of substantial material such as thick, stiff leather or rubber, not of lightweight material such as canvas or nylon. Thickness is the most important feature. Special boots and chaps made of (ostensibly) snake-proof fabric are also available.

☛ Trousers worn on the outside, not tucked into boots. The loose cloth will interfere with fang penetration.

☛ Shorts, bare feet, sandals, and even nylon athletic shoes provide little to no protection against bites.

What Were They Doing When the Snake Bit?

The following list is a self-explanatory indicator of behaviors to avoid if you want to prevent a venomous bite (excluding handling or harassing snakes—when you're just asking for trouble). (Klauber, 1997, p. 962-3)

☛ Crawling through brush or under a fence	22.5%
☛ Climbing among rocks	18.0%
☛ Walking with inadequate foot or leg coverings	12.0%
☛ Going barefoot in the open	11.0%
☛ Gathering firewood after dark	9.0%
☛ Reaching into hollow logs, heavy grass, or brush; under stones; into holes	5.0%
☛ Snakes encountered in camps	3.5%
☛ Bitten through "snake-proof" footwear	2.0%
☛ Unknown circumstances	17.0%

Unfortunately, children at play rank high in the statistical lists of those bitten. This is likely due in part to the fact that children have no natural or instinctive fear of snakes. What is also unfortunate is that by the time they reach adulthood, most people will likely have a totally disproportionate fear of all snakes that will incapacitate their ability to react with common sense in real encounters.

Fight or Flight

If you should trigger a coiling response from a copperhead lying about, know that the snake is still just as likely to retreat as it is to attack. Most experts with broad field knowledge agree that most snakes attempt to escape rather than do battle. After all, energy, and perhaps venom, spent on you is that much less to use in the search for supper.

Factors Affecting the Seriousness of a Snake Bite

Many agents interact to make the impact of a bite difficult to predict. They include:

{ reptiles & amphibians }

- Age, size, sex, vigor, and health of the victim.
- Victim's susceptibility to protein poisoning, which includes the number of previous bites that might provide partial immunity.
- Emotional condition of the victim. Fear will increase heart rate and thus aid the distribution of venom throughout the body.
- Location of the bite, which is less serious in the extremities or in fatty tissue.
- Nature of the bite; for example, a direct hit with both fangs fully embedded or a glancing blow or scratch.
- Protection afforded by clothing—thicker is better.
- Number of bites—two or more are not unheard of.
- Length of hold time for the actual bite.
- Emotional state of the snake. If hurt or violently excited, it is likely to inject more venom.
- Species, age, and size of the snake.
- Condition of the venom glands—were they recently depleted?
- Condition of the fangs—broken, renewed, due for shedding?
- Bacterial microorganisms in the snake's mouth that contribute to infection.
- Nature of first-aid treatment.

Signs and Symptoms of Envenomation

Fang marks may be present as one or more well-defined punctures or as a series of small lacerations or scratches, or there may not be any noticeable or obvious markings where the bite occurred. The absence of fang marks does not preclude the possibility of a bite (especially if a juvenile snake is involved). However, with adult pit viper envenomation, fang marks are invariably present and are generally seen on close examination. Bleeding may persist from the fang wounds. On the other hand, the presence of fang marks does not always indicate envenomation. Sometimes venom is conserved or is already largely spent on the efforts of a recent hunt.

Venomous snakes do not always inject venom, particularly when they strike in defense or when startled. However, if you are bitten by a venomous snake, you should seek treatment immediately and not wait for the signs and symptoms of envenomation to appear. The specific indications and symptoms that may manifest themselves in a victim who has been envenomated can vary considerably in presence and in severity. The time of development will also vary considerably from case to case. Signs and symptoms of cases of crotalid envenomation—including copperheads—may include some of the following. Not all of these symptoms will necessarily develop, even with severe envenomation.

Frequency of Bite Sign or Symptom Occurrence

Pain: 65–95%	Decreased hemoglobin: 37%
Swelling, edema: 74%	Thirst: 34%
Weakness: 72%	Change in body temperature: 31%
Pulse rate changes: 60%	Local tissue death (necrosis): 27%
Numbness, tingling: 63%	Abnormal electrocardiogram: 26%
Increased blood clotting time: 39%	Abnormal amounts of sugar in the urine (glycosuria): 20%
Faintness, dizziness: 57%	Increased salivation: 20%
Escape of blood into tissues from ruptured blood vessels (ecchymosis): 51%	Bluish discoloration of the skin (cyanosis):16%
Nausea and/or vomiting: 48%	Sweating and/or chills: 64%
Excess protein in the urine (proteinuria): 16%	Presence of blood in the urine (hematuria): 15%
Increased blood platelets: 4%	Unconsciousness: 12%
Decreased blood platelets: 42%	Blurring of vision: 12%
Muscle twitches and contractions (fasciculations): 41%	Numbness, tingling in the affected part: 42%
Blisters (vesicles or boils): 40%	Swollen eyelid: 2%
Regional lymph adenopathy: 40%	Retinal hemorrhage: 2%
Respiratory rate changes: 40%	Convulsions: 1%

If You Are Bitten

SNAKEBITE TREATMENT: In the simplest possible terms, treatment consists of the following:

☛ Get the victim to the hospital or treatment center as soon as possible.

☛ Administer the appropriate antidote (antivenin).

Findlay Russell, a global authority on snakebites, counsels, "If you haven't done anything except get to a hospital, you haven't done anything wrong." (Rubio, 1998, p. 147)

In cases of serious pit viper envenomation, intravenous fluid resuscitation is also important. Of course, proper medical treatment and management of a venomous snakebite is both involved and complex. Fortunately, pertinent considerations and treatment protocols are only a click away at webmd.com if your ER doc lacks experience. Antivenin, likewise, is available at most hospitals and possibly even at larger drugstores.

{ reptiles & amphibians }

CONCERNING THE SNAKE: Make sure that the responsible snake or snakes have been appropriately and safely contained and prevented from inflicting any additional bites. Try to identify (not catch) the offending snake. If you are bitten in the U.S. or Canada and cannot identify the snake, don't worry. More than 99 percent of all snakebites (excluding bites by nonindigenous species in collections or zoos) are by pit vipers, and the same antivenin is used for treatment regardless of the offending pit viper species (though some bites may require more antivenin than others). Bites from coral snakes, which require a different antivenin, are so rare and the snake so easily identified and differentiated from a pit viper that there's little chance the attending physician will confuse the treatment.

In a characteristic understatement, Dr. Robert E. Arnold acknowledges the impulse for revenge when he writes: "Do not waste time hunting for the snake! Personal reasons may prompt one to find the snake and kill it, but this should be done after the victim is on the way to the hospital. Please do not feel constrained to present the reptile remains to the doctor or hospital for viewing. First, the snake may not be dead and may recover at an inopportune moment. Second, few physicians are able to identify most snakes. Third, it makes no difference what kind of snake it is since only one pit viper antivenin is available."

Note, however, that a second kind of antivenin has become available. Its market name is CroFab (Crotalidae Polyvalent Immune Fab [Ovine]), and it was approved by the FDA in October 2000 as an effective agent for minimal and moderate crotalid envenomation. It is less likely to cause anaphylaxis, an allergic reaction that can be very serious. Prompt (within six hours of snakebite) treatment with CroFab is recommended. CroFab has been well received by physicians because of its efficacy and safety profile. This has encouraged doctors to treat more bite victims, including patients with milder bites, as well as to start treatment with CroFab earlier in the course of poisoning to reduce its severity.

TRANSPORTATION: Arrange immediately for transportation of the victim to the nearest emergency room or treatment center. Calling 911 is often the best strategy. Although venomous snakebite is a medical emergency, it is not so dire as to warrant a hair-raising dash to the hospital at excessive speeds. Except in a tiny number of cases (where the bite is to the head, neck, or torso), you have time for a sane, controlled drive to the nearest emergency room. If possible, call the ER to let them know you are coming with a snakebite victim.

WILDERNESS SITUATIONS: The objective is to get to a hospital and antivenin as quickly as possible. Generally speaking, you want to be very still after being bitten because activity accelerates the spread of the venom. In a remote area, however, obtaining treatment expeditiously is more important than being still, so you'll want to set off toward help, adverse effects of movement notwithstanding.

When walking to find help, head for the closest road, house, phone, or site of known human habitation. If alternative routes are available, choose the one that requires the least aerobic exertion, even if it is a little longer. If you are in the wilderness, do not compound your problems by leaving the trail and getting lost. Continue on the trail in the direction most likely to lead to help. Depart from the trail only if a road or house comes into view and you are certain you can reach it.

You may have some very tough decisions to make. What if you encounter a person who is willing to assist? Do you send them ahead to find help while you remain still, or do you continue plugging along? Every such decision must be made in the context of which alternative will get you to professional medical help soonest.

WILDERNESS EVACUATIONS: There are very few endeavors as strenuous as carrying a person over a trail or cross-country. The safe evacuation of a nonambulatory person in the wilderness requires at least six and preferably eight or more persons. When fewer than six able people are present, it is almost always more prudent to go for help than to attempt evacuation.

The Great Snakebite First Aid Controversy

You should know that the preferred first aid for snakebite has changed a number of times during the past several decades. Gone are the days of making "X" incisions over the fang marks, applying tourniquets, sucking venom from the wound with your mouth, packing the bitten limb in ice, or plying the victim with whiskey.

Mayoclinic.com recommends if a snake bites you:
- ☞ Remain calm.
- ☞ Immobilize the bitten arm or leg and stay as quiet as possible to keep the poison from spreading through your body.
- ☞ Remove jewelry before you start to swell.
- ☞ Position yourself, if possible, so that the bite is at or below the level of your heart.
- ☞ Cleanse the wound, but don't flush it with water, and cover it with a clean, dry dressing.
- ☞ Apply a splint to reduce movement of the affected area, but keep it loose enough so as not to restrict blood flow.
- ☞ Don't use a tourniquet or apply ice.

{ reptiles & amphibians }

Massasauga Rattlesnake
(Sistrurus catenatus)

- Massasauga rattlesnakes are potentially lethal, but because they are an endangered species in Illinois, encounters are highly unlikely. The fact that massasaugas are in serious decline is a warning bell telling us that something is wrong.

- Mature snakes can range from 18 to 39 inches. Key characteristics include: nine large symmetrical plates on top of head; elliptical pupil; pit between eye and nostril; light-edged dark blotches on back and sides; rattle or horny button on tail tip; four head stripes; back scales strongly keeled; anal plate not divided. Black belly with irregular white or yellow markings. Newborn tail tip yellow, but darkens with age.

- Massasaugas live in wet areas including in prairies, marshes, and low areas along rivers and lakes. In many areas massasaugas also use adjacent uplands during part of the year. They often hibernate in crayfish burrows but they may also be found under logs and tree roots or in small mammal burrows. Unlike other rattlesnakes, massasaugas hibernate alone.

- Like all rattlesnakes, massasaugas bear live young. The young actually hatch from eggs while still in the female's body. Depending on the health of the individual, adult females may bear young every year or every other year. When food is especially scarce, they may only have young every three years. Massasaugas that have young every year, mate in the spring and bear their young in late summer or early fall. In contrast, snakes that have young every other year, mate in autumn and bear young the next summer. Litter size varies from 5 to 19 young.

- The massasauga plays an important role in its ecosystems, both as a predator on small mammals, other snakes, and amphibians and as prey for hawks, owls, cranes, and some mammals.

- Massasaugas are docile, secretive snakes that will try to escape rather than fight. But they will protect themselves and may bite if cornered. Be cautious in massasauga areas by wearing leather boots or shoes, watching where you place your hands and feet and walking around, rather than over, fallen logs. Treat massasaugas with respect, like any wild animal. If you are bitten by a massasauga, seek medical help immediately.

MASSASAUGA
RATTLESNAKE

- Don't cut the wound or attempt to remove the venom.
- Don't drink caffeine or alcohol.
- Don't try to capture the snake, but try to remember its color and shape so you can describe it, which will help in your treatment.
- Call 911 or seek immediate medical attention, especially if the area changes color, begins to swell, or is painful.

CONCERNING THE VICTIM: Additionally, universally approved, noncontroversial first aid includes the following:

- With a pen, mark the border of advancing swelling every 15 minutes.
- Reassure the victim.

What Not to Do If Bitten:

- Do not eat or drink anything unless directed or approved by medical sources.
- Do not engage in strenuous physical activity.
- Do not apply oral (mouth) suction to bite.
- Do not cut into or incise bite marks with a blade.
- Do not drink any alcohol or use any medication.
- Do not apply either hot or cold packs.
- Do not apply a tourniquet or use sticks or other hard objects for splints.
- Do not use a stun gun or electric shock of any kind.

{ reptiles & amphibians }

☞ Do not give antivenin in the field because of the risk of severe allergic complications.

The primary and essential treatment for venomous snakebite is the administration of the appropriate antivenin by a trained physician. All of the foregoing first aid procedures are intended to minimize the effects of envenomation until professional medical treatment can be obtained.

*Remember, Ace bandages or other wide bandaging must not be wrapped so tightly as to cut off systemic venous or arterial circulation. Properly applied, such bandages will *not* compromise the systemic circulation.

WHAT TO TELL THEM AT THE HOSPITAL: Because venomous snakebite is rare, it's possible that the attending physician knows little or nothing about snakebite management. Our recommendation is to directly question the physician concerning his experience with snakebite. You can also tactfully ask staff to use physician consultants available through Poison Control (aapcc.org).

The Most Important Things to Know about All Venomous Snakes

In the general populace, fear of venomous snakes far outstrips understanding or even appreciation of their place in the natural order. Though potentially lethal when trespassed upon, they mind their own business and still are often deprived of habitat and respect, not to mention compassion. The subject of many myths, venomous snakes in particular are worthy of our study and contemplation—for our sake, as well as theirs.

Laurence M. Klauber wrote eloquently of the rattlesnake, but his words have a broader application to all venomous snakes:

Of all these myths, that which has most deeply affected human impressions and attitudes toward rattlesnakes is the one that pictures these snakes as malignant, vindictive, and crafty, with an especial hatred of mankind. Recently a radio commentator called rattlesnakes the "symbol of pure evil."

But a rattlesnake is only a primitive creature with rudimentary perceptions and reactions. Dangerous it surely is, and I hold no brief for its survival except in remote areas where its capacity to destroy harmful rodents may be exercised without danger to man or his domestic animals. But that the rattlesnake bears an especial enmity toward man is mythical. It seeks only to defend itself from injury by intruders of superior size, of which man is one. It could not, through the ages, have developed any especial enmity

160

for man, since the first human being any rattlesnake may encoun-
ter is the usually the last. (Klauber, 1997, p. 1291)

TURTLES

Turtles embrace "a philosophy of meditation and passive resistance," mused esteemed biologist Archie Carr in his enduring 1952 *Handbook of Turtles*. "The magnetism of turtle personality stems more from good-humored quaintness and elfin drollery than from intellectuality," Carr added with nonscientific yet true affection.

Biting Back

Indeed, many of us do find these 200 million-year-old reptiles of the *Testudines* order irresistible, and most turtles are harmless and charming. Their appeal figures prominently in the great Hindu and Native American creation mythologies, and they have been esteemed in Greece and China for millennia. A few species, however, would make venerable University of Tennessee Lady Vols basketball coach Pat Summitt proud. Pat preaches "Defense! Defense! Defense!"— a strategy that the biting and the "stink bombing" turtles have mastered.

Turtles have no teeth, but they do have beaks with hard, sharp edges for cutting food. Some are capable of surprising neck extensions and, even more surprising, lightning-quick striking speed. Put all this under one shell, and you have the legendary snapping turtles known for their irascibility and aggressively defensive responses.

Snapping turtles are among the largest of the freshwater turtles, with lengths up to 26 inches for the alligator snapping species and 18.5 inches for the common snapping turtle, each of which sports an imposing, truly prehistoric-looking head and commanding jaws. The snapping turtle likes to rest in warm shallows and often burrows in the mud, leaving only its nostrils and eyes exposed, poised to "snap" up some prey. Both species of snappers are highly aquatic. The common snapper rarely basks, and the alligator snapper never basks. The alligator snapper will be found on the bottom of the water body, likely with its mouth agape to attract fish by wiggling a pinkish, worm-like part of its tongue. If you see an alligator snapper on land, she is very likely a nesting female.

The snapper family is found in the eastern two-thirds of the U.S. In the more northern reaches, the turtles do hibernate, but there are reports of common snappers moving under the ice in the middle of New England winters. For this reason you should not automatically assume that snappers are dormant in the chillier months.

{ reptiles & amphibians }

Snapping Turtle (*Chelydra serpentina*)

- The snapper has an extremely powerful bite, and is much more prone to bite on land where it is known for repeated attacks with elevated hindquarters that launch a forward lunge. Any bite, no matter how small, should be washed with antibacterial soap and dressed appropriately. Because snappers eat carrion (among other things) and thereby carry bacteria, seek professional medical assistance. Formidable claws may also make deep scratches.

- The common snapper's natural range extends from southeastern Canada, southwest to the edge of the Rocky Mountains, as far east as Nova Scotia and Florida and as far southwest as northeastern Mexico.

- These turtles can range in size from 8 to 18.5 inches, but generally mature to 15 inches. Average weight is 10 to 35 pounds, but a record wild catch weighed 75 pounds.

- A massive primordial head with powerful hooked jaws and a long tail (equal in length to the carapace) with "sawtooth" ridges dominate the appearance. A long neck with brown to yellow skin enables an impressive reach to bite. The carapace (upper shell) is oval, and tan to dark brown or almost black.

- Snapping turtles feed on snails, vegetation, frogs, toads, young waterfowl, smaller turtles, fish, mussels, crayfish, snakes, and carrion.

- The snapping turtle emerges from its winter retreat and mates from April to November, with peak egg-laying activity in June. Females are not known for maternal protection of nests.

- Though they are sometimes found in brackish environments, these turtles prefer freshwater with muddy bottoms and plentiful vegetation, including shallow ponds, streams, canals, and the edges of lakes or rivers.

- Notoriously cranky, especially on land, the snapper is active day and night. It is a highly aquatic animal and an excellent swimmer that prefers to spend its time resting in warm shallows, buried in the mud with nostrils and eyes exposed. When disturbed in the water it will likely try to swim away quietly rather than retaliate as it does with relentless vigor on land. While it generally hibernates from November to April in a muskrat lodge, under a mud bank overhang, or under vegetative debris, it may also be active during the colder months.

ANGRY
SNAPPING
TURTLE

Sensing Trouble

Turtles avoid danger by sensing vibration, relying more on this touch sensitivity than they do on their other senses. Snapping turtles will try to depart the scene if threatened, so the danger to swimmers, boaters, and people who are fishing is minimal. Snappers will, however, try to steal fishing bait or caught fish hung on stringers. In this case, it's best to cut the line rather than tangle with the snapper's "business end." Waders, especially children who might like to creep along any permanent freshwater or even brackish shores, would do well to be wearing shoes as a general practice to avoid cans and glass, if nothing else. Generally, though, if accidentally stepped on in the water, snappers will behave rather well and just pull in their heads. They rarely if ever bite people underwater.

No Teasing or Squeezing

Snapping turtles on land, however, are definitely reptiles to be respected. Most harmful encounters are initiated by people who try to tease or capture a snapping turtle. When a serious bite is inflicted, it is hard to blame the turtle, which is most likely suspended out of its element, upside down, held by its tail. It is important to note that, according to Carr and reptile expert Ross Allen, the damage done to the tail vertebrae from lifting a large alligator snapper, that can weigh up to 150 pounds or more, by the tail eventually kills it. This also applies to heavier common snappers. If you *must* carry a large alligator snapper, hold it across and well in front of your body with a grasp on its upper shell behind

{ reptiles & amphibians }

163

the head and above the tail. Common snappers should be grasped with both hands holding the back end of the carapace, or upper shell. Either method still will leave you vulnerable, especially to the menacing claws.

For smaller specimens, carry the animal by the base of the tail with the plastron, or underside, toward your body.

Attitude

Legends of amputated feet are exaggerated, but snapping turtles are quick, agile, powerful, and not to be messed with. The alligator snapper is less testy, but still a fearsome match for any human. One report offers that "when handled, the alligator snapper does not make violent striking movements like the common snapper but stays remarkably still with the mouth wide open . . . though it does stretch round to bite any part of its handler that is held within reach."

The Georgia Wildlife Federation offers this caution: "If the common snapping turtle is pestered while on land, it will repeatedly try to bite. . . . Even a small snapper can inflict a painful wound with its hooked beak. If handled, which is definitely not recommended, be very careful . . . Because a well-placed bite from the common snapping turtle can sever a few fingers at one time."

Common snappers have a reputation for tenacity, as well as ferocity. Artist David Carroll, who beached one to draw it, recalled that "a snapping turtle cornered on land, or in shallow water with no escape route, will keep turning in a tight circle to face any challenger, with neck and legs set for a strike and jaws slightly apart. These creatures will not back down."

If a turtle bites you, use common sense by cleaning the wound, applying antiseptic, and seeking medical attention. Snapping turtles eat carrion, among other things, so the risk of infection from a bite is a real one.

Turtle Safety Precautions

☞ Wear shoes when wading.
☞ Do not engage snapping turtles to risk the danger of bites, claw marks, or odor release. Snapping turtles, especially, are most prone to attack when handled or cornered on land.
☞ If you are bitten or scratched, wash the wound with disinfectant and seek medical attention.
☞ If a snapping turtle takes your bait or lure, it's best to cut the line rather than "tango" with the turtle.
☞ If you must carry a snapping turtle, carry small animals by the base of the tail with the plastron, underside, facing but well away from your leg. For larger alligator snappers, grasp them by the shell above the head and tail and carry them in front of you well away

from your body. For common snappers, grasp them by the back of the carapace with both hands. Carrying larger specimens by the tail will eventually kill them.

TOADS

Shout it from the highest toadstool: "Warts and all—especially if you don't want even more insects—you gotta love toads." These amphibian changelings of the Anura order are critical in helping to manage the perpetually thriving insect population. With a few minor exceptions, toads are generally not harmful to humans. Dogs and cats, however, sometimes have lethal run-ins.

Warts?

Yes and no. Yes, the surface of a toad's skin is described as "warty," but no, you can't catch warts from handling them. Warts have viral causes, and although a toad's rough body texture looks like it might be dangerous, the worst that can happen if you handle them is an allergic reaction with runny eyes and nose. But if you try to eat them . . . .

They Leave a Really Bad Taste in Your Mouth

Toads have an enlarged pair of parotid glands situated on various locations on their cranial crests (depending on the species). These glands secret a viscous, white poison into the mouths of predators. An inflamed mouth and throat, nausea, irregular heartbeat, and in some cases, death, discourage or prevent a second helping of toad.

Doggie Downers and Kitty Killers

Dogs, and less frequently cats, seem to have a hard time resisting this easy prey. According to the *Journal of Venomous Animals and Toxins*, "Dogs can be envenomated biting or ingesting the toad that secretes the poison in the oral mucous of the predator. The effects of the toad venom are, mainly, cardiotoxic in nature. In 1935, a child died in Hawaii after having ingested a toad hunted by its father in a sugar cane field. . . . chemical composition of the toad venom is very complex and varied among the species belonging to this genus. . . . The effects of the venom appear almost immediately after envenomation."

Symptoms of Dangerous Toad and Pet Encounters

☞ The degree of symptoms depends upon the amount of toxin absorbed. Basic symptoms are:

EASTERN
AMERICAN TOAD

☛ Immediate and heavy drooling that can sometimes be foamy.
☛ Head shaking as though the dog or cat is trying to rid itself of a sensation.
☛ Crying.
☛ With moderate toxin ingestion, uncoordinated movement and staggering will be evident.
☛ In more severe situations, the animal cannot walk or stand.
☛ In the most extreme cases, convulsions and death can occur.

Other conditions may trigger similar symptoms, so try to ascertain whether the dog or cat has ingested a toad. A history of the pet's playing with a toad is helpful information.

Pet First Aid

If you know or strongly suspect that your dog or cat has been poisoned by a toad, *immediately* flush out your pet's mouth with water, rinsing for approximately five minutes. The use of a garden hose for continuous flow is advisable, provided you are careful not to choke or drown the animal. Extreme care should be taken that the animal does not swallow the rinse water.

NO KISSING, NO KIDDING

It's true that toads do secrete fluids from their skins, and that some people are allergic to these secretions. Some allergic reactions occur after skin contact, but most are brought on by mucous membrane contact. Therefore, after handling toads or frogs it's wise not to touch your mouth, nose, or eyes until after you have washed your hands with soap.

Eastern American Toad (Bufo americanus)

- Skin secretions are irritating to mucous membranes and may prove fatal to dogs and cats, especially if the animal is ingested. Even if you think no secretions have been released after handling an American toad, refrain from touching your eyes, nose, or mouth until you wash your hands well with soap.
- American toads are abundant throughout Illinois.
- These toads are 2 to 3 inches long with a recorded maximum length of more than 4.25 inches.
- They are olive, brown, or brick red with assorted patterning in lighter colors, but may also appear almost as plain brown. Belly is usually spotted and a light stripe may run down the middle of the back. Parotid glands do not touch the prominent cranial crest.
- American toads are hearty eaters, especially of insects and some other invertebrates.
- They breed in shallow bodies of water (ditches, shallow streams, temporary pools of standing water) from March to July, leaving egg strings attached to vegetation.
- The American toad makes its home wherever abundant insects and moisture can be found, including domestic sites such as suburban yards, around water spigots next to houses, and in wilderness areas including mountainous forests.
- This toad is generally, but not exclusively, nocturnal. It does not bite or attack, avoids contact, and is "passively aggressive" only through release of skin secretion.

Have your veterinarian give specific antidotes by injection as soon as possible, especially when there is any doubt about how severely poisoned your pet may be. Remember, too, that the smaller the dog or cat, the greater the possibility of serious toxicity. Since many toad poisonings occur in the evening or nighttime hours, call your nearest animal emergency clinic for assistance.

Poison Protection?

Probably because it undergoes a radical transformation, beginning life as a water-bound tadpole that drops its tail, grows legs, and then lives on land, the toad figures heavily in fairly tale and legend. One such

{ reptiles & amphibians }

legend is the "toadstone." This is "a stone or similar object held to have formed in the head or body of a toad often worn as a charm or an antidote to poison." Don't bet on it.

Toad and Frog Safety Precautions

It is unlikely that you or your children will have adverse reactions from handling toads. However, handling generally produces stress in the animals and will likely cause them to release secretions to which you may be allergic.

☞ If you do handle frogs or toads, wash your hands thoroughly before touching your nose, eyes, or mouth (and certainly before eating). This applies even if you do not think that the animal has discharged any fluid.

☞ If you suspect your dog or cat has bitten or eaten a toad or a frog, rinse its mouth with water and rush the animal to the vet. Death can occur within 30 to 60 minutes after ingestion.

birds

Birds, you say, really? Birds are dangerous? Are we in the classic Alfred Hitchcock movie *The Birds* with Tippi Hedren freaking out after a swarm? No, but there are a couple of very large birds to whom you want to give a very wide berth: Canada geese and swans. And there's histoplasmosis, a fungal infection, to talk about, too.

SWANS

On April 16, 2012, a tragedy occurred when a swan attacked 37-year-old expert swimmer Anthony Hensley, who worked for a company that used swans and dogs to keep geese away from properties on a Des Plaines pond. Hensley, who reportedly enjoyed working with animals, drowned when he was overwhelmed in his kayak by an aggressive swan. Most likely the bird was an often-seen mute swan (*Cygnus olor*), one of Illinois' three swan species including the trumpeter swan (*Cygnus buccinator*) and the tundra swan (*Cygnus columbianus*).

Swans can weigh up to 33 pounds and have a wingspan of 8 feet. They can be formidably aggressive, especially when their nest is threatened.

MUTE SWAN

All of these swans are found in the Chicago area, but the mute swan is the one to beware of, since it can be aggressive toward humans.

TRUMPETER SWAN

TUNDRA SWAN

Mute swan (*Cygnus olor*)

- These birds can be very aggressive, especially during spring mating season. Physical and emotional trauma or even death can result from hostile encounters.
- This species ranges from 4 to nearly 6 feet in length and has an 8-to-9-foot wingspan. Males can weigh up to 33 pounds.
- This large swan's plumage is totally white. It has a long S-shaped neck with an orange bill bordered with black. It is recognizable by the pronounced knob atop its bill.
- They fly with necks extended with regular, slow wing beats.
- Mute swans nest on large mounds that they build with water-side vegetation in shallow water on islands in the middle or at the very edge of a lake. They are monogamous and often reuse the same nest each year, restoring or rebuilding it as needed. Male and female swans share the care of the nest,
- They feed on a wide range of vegetation, both submerged aquatic plants, which they reach with their long necks, and by grazing on land. The food commonly includes agricultural crop plants such as oilseed rape and wheat. Feeding flocks in the winter may cause significant crop damage, often as much through trampling with their large webbed feet as through direct consumption.
- The name "mute" derives from it being less vocal than other swan species.

Reports document that swans have even killed geese by holding them underwater. Swan aggression certainly extends to humans, and you should avoid contact, including feeding, with the birds—even though they are temptingly beautiful.

Mute swans (*Cygnus olor*) are a species of bird intentionally introduced for their aesthetic appeal from Western Europe. Between the years of 1910 and 1912, over 500 mute swans were imported. While most of the captive mute swans in New England had their flight feathers clipped, a small number of birds escaped from captivity. By the late 1960s, populations of feral mute swans were recorded in Pennsylvania, Maryland, Delaware, and Virginia, thus severely affecting the Chesapeake Bay watershed. Established populations in the Great Lakes and the Long Island Sound are causing extensive damage to the freshwater and brackish ecosystems.

{ birds }

CANADA GEESE*

Most of the information below is taken from the Ohio Division of Wildlife's online information. Gratitude is here expressed.

Canada geese are probably the most adaptable and tolerant of all native waterfowl. They are also considered North America's most populous water birds. If left undisturbed, they will readily establish nesting territories on any suitable pond, be it located on a farm, backyard, golf course, apartment or condominium complex, or city park. After years of steady growth, the population of giant Canada geese in Illinois has remained flat at around 107,000 birds over the last decade, according to an annual helicopter survey by the Illinois Department of Natural Resources.

No Snacks Allowed

Many people will welcome and start feeding the first pair of geese on their pond, but these geese will soon wear out their welcome. In just a few years, a pair of geese can easily become 50 to 100 birds. The feces will foul the areas around the pond and surrounding yards and also damage the lawn, pond, and other vegetation. DO NOT FEED GEESE. Geese that are fed will lose their fear of humans and attack adults, children, and pets during the nesting season (March through June). Feeding bread, corn, potato chips, popcorn, and other human food items harms the geese and trains the geese to attack people for food. Feeding popcorn, bread, or shelled corn is like feeding a child junk food since the geese are not receiving a balanced diet. This activity is a very selfish pursuit when only one party, humans, derives a benefit—the joy and excitement of close interaction with a wild creature.

When Geese Lose Their Fear of Humans

Geese that are fed by well-meaning people lose their natural fear and reside closer than normal to humans. This can lead to violent attacks during the nesting season, especially to people who are afraid of geese. It's fairly easy to be afraid of an aggressive male Canada goose defending its young. They charge you with a flapping 4-to-6-foot wingspan. After the hissing comes biting. Documented goose attacks on humans have caused serious physical injury, such as broken bones and head injuries, and emotional distress. Many of these injuries have occurred when the person tried to avoid an attack and tripped over an object (such as steps, curbs, and planters). Parks, businesses, apartment or condo associations may be held legally liable for physical or psychological

No, not significantly, according to scientific studies. Canada geese do make a mess of things, dropping feathers and scat around their areas of habitation. The mess, however, is more of a visual problem than a bacterial one. It almost goes without saying: don't let your kids play in poop!

damages. Thus, the goose-feeding creates justifiable public health and safety concerns for people, too.

For some the thought of being afraid of birds is ludicrous, but for those who have to endure repeated attacks as they enter and exit their place of work, for example, there is another perspective. Tippi Hedren, star of the above-mentioned movie *The Birds*, was promised the birds in close attack would be mechanical. They were not. In a state of exhaustion, when one of the birds gouged her cheek and narrowly missed her eye, Hedren sat down on the set and began crying. A physician ordered a week's rest, which Hedren said at the time was riddled with "nightmares filled with flapping wings."

If a Goose Attacks You

☞ Waterfowl have excellent vision. Geese seem to pay very close attention to the eyes and body language of humans and other animals. An encounter with an aggressive goose can usually be resolved if you maintain direct eye contact while facing your body directly towards the attacking goose.

☞ If the goose acts aggressively, calmly and slowly back away, watching for obstacles.

☞ Maintain a neutral demeanor (do not yell, swing, kick, or act hostile). Extreme aggression may cause the female to join the confrontation, which usually causes an even more aggressive attack from the male.

☞ Never turn your back or shoulders away from the hostile goose, and never close or squint your eyes or block your eyes with a purse or briefcase.

☞ If the goose makes an aggressive move towards you while hissing or spreading out its wings, you should slowly back away while using your peripheral vision to watch for obstacles you could trip over.

☞ Do not cower, hide your face, turn your back, or run from the goose.

☞ If a goose flies up towards your face, then duck or move away at a 90-degree angle to the direction of flight, still facing the attacking goose.

{ birds }

175

Canada Goose (Branta Canadensis)

- These birds can be very aggressive, especially during spring mating season. Physical and emotional trauma can result from hostile encounters.
- This species ranges from 30 to 43 inches in length and has a 50-to-73-inch wingspan. Males weigh 7-to-14 pounds, with females slightly less.
- These geese have a black head and neck, white patches on the face, and a brownish-gray body. The black head and neck with white "chinstrap" distinguish the Canada goose from all other goose species.
- Canada geese are primarily herbivores, although they sometimes eat small insects and fish. Their diet includes green vegetation and grains. In the water, they feed from silt at the bottom of the body of water. They also feed on aquatic plants, such as seaweeds. In urban areas, they are also known to pick food out of garbage bins.
- Their nests are usually located in an elevated area near water, such as streams, lakes, ponds, and sometimes on a beaver lodge. Their eggs are laid in a shallow depression lined with plant material and down.
- This species is native to North America. It breeds in Canada and the northern United States in a variety of habitats.
- As 2-year-olds, these geese mate for life and produce goslings every spring.
- These geese are also renowned for their V-shaped flight formation and their haunting honk as they fly. The front flying position is rotated because it consumes the most energy.

Deterring Nests

If you have a body of water that naturally attracts Canada geese, one measure you can take is to allow the grass to grow up at least 12 inches high on the perimeter of the water. This discourages the birds from nesting and gaining easy entry to the water. Conversely, shortly mowing the same grass right down to the water line is akin to hanging out a Holiday Inn sign for the geese.

Good Riddance

Canada geese are protected under the Federal Migratory Bird Treaty Act. This protection extends to the geese, goslings, nests, and eggs. Nonlethal scare and hazing tactics, which do not harm the geese, are allowed. These tactics include: pyrotechnics, dogs, barriers, a grid on the pond, laser pointers (at night), distress calls, or grape-flavored repellants such as Flight Control.

If nonlethal tactics have been used in the past without success, the Division of Wildlife may issue a lethal permit to allow the landowner to destroy nests, conduct a goose roundup, or shoot geese. These permits can only be used March 1 through August 31.

Histoplasmosis

Histoplasmosis is a disease caused by the fungus *Histoplasma capsulatum,* which grows in soil and material contaminated with bat or bird droppings. Soil contamination occurs after three consecutive years of large flock roostings. Starlings (*Sturnus vulgaris*) are a typical source for contaminations. (They are also a tale of human interference gone awry. Eugene Schieffelin, president of the infamous American Acclimatization Society, tried to introduce every bird species mentioned in the works of William Shakespeare to North America. He introduced 60 starlings into New York's Central Park in 1890. The offspring of the original 60 starlings have thrived. There are now an estimated 150 million in the United States, and they are generally considered a nuisance.) Spores become airborne when contaminated soil is disturbed. Breathing the spores causes infection.

Please refer to the mammals chapter, page 45, for more information about histoplasmosis.

{ birds }

CANADA GOOSE
GOSLING

CANADA GEESE

A FLOCK OF STARLINGS
(SEE HISTOPLASMOSIS)

STARLING

flora

A FLOCK OF STARLINGS
(SEE HISTOPLASMOSIS).

STARLING

For all the splendid variety of the plant world that nourishes us, both body and soul, there are a surprising number of species that are variously toxic to ingest. Others are skin irritants such as poison ivy. These are the only two ways to get in trouble with plants: ingesting them (including inhalation) and touching them. Having said that, the paths to those troubles are not always as clearly marked as you might think, and the consequences of veering off the safe course may prove extremely aggravating or even lethal. It's one thing to set yourself purposefully before a final serving of deadly nightshade berries with a perfectly chilled, exceptional chardonnay, and it's another to experiment with some mysterious but noxious mushrooms that might well send you "knock, knock, knockin' on heaven's door."

TO INGEST OR NOT TO INGEST: IS THAT THE QUESTION?

No, it isn't the question. ***Never even consider eating vegetation you are not familiar with, especially wild mushrooms of any kind.*** From azaleas to yew trees, the natural world has many species that can prove mildly or lethally injurious to you and your pets. Reactions can include severe vomiting; slow or irregular heartbeat; blurred vision; inability to urinate; convulsions; coma; and death, among many others. It is especially important to teach your children never to put a plant in their mouths without first asking an adult if that plant is safe. As is so often the case, children can find danger in the most unlikely places. A child can become seriously ill from biting into a daffodil bulb or drinking the water out of a vase holding a bunch of lilies of the valley.

Flora Toxic to Ingest

The following incomplete inventory indicates the number of common flora species that are potentially harmful for you (or your pets) to ingest. The point of this partial list is to indicate that there are many dangers in the plant kingdom and to encourage you strongly to refrain from "just tasting." I'm not trying to put you at odds with the natural world, but it is easy to be misled by plants—one part may be edible while another is poisonous, and there are no obvious rules of thumb.

Take tomatoes for example. Their red luscious fruit is loved all over the world, but ingesting their leaves can make you ill. The potato tuber is another world staple, but again the green parts of the plant can make you sick. *Venomous Animals and Poisonous Plants*, a Peterson Field Guide, by Steven Foster and Roger Caras is a good reference for those curious to learn more about which parts of which plants are dangerous. Again, we list these species here as a signpost that plants are not to be casually ingested.

All the plants or trees on this list do not spell "d-e-a-t-h," but some do, and all will generate various degrees of discomfort based on the amount ingested and the condition (age, size, general health) of the person who has eaten them. Some species on this list may also be medicinal or forage plants under some circumstances, at some dose, but that's a decision best left to the experts, given the risks involved.

American nightshade *(Solanum americanum)*
Atamasco lily *(Zephyranthes atamasco)*
Azalea *(Rhododendron* spp.*)**
Avocado *(Persea americanca)**

Barilla *(Halogeton glomeratus)*
Black locust *(Robinia pseudoacacia)*
Black nightshade *(Solanum nigrum)*
Blue-green algae *(Cyanophyta spp.)*
Bracken fern *(Pteridium aquilinum)*
Buckeyes *(Aeseulus spp.)**
Bunchflower *(Melanthium spp.)*
Caladium *(Caladium spp.)**
Carolina all-spice or bubby bush *(Calycanthus floridus)**
Castorbean *(Ricinus communis)*
Chinaberry tree *(Melia azedarach)*
Chokeberry *(Prunus spp.)*
Climbing nightshade *(Solanum dulcamara)* known in Illinois as bittersweet nightshade
Cocklebur *(Xanthium spp.)*
Coral beam *(Erythrina herbacea)*
Crow poison *(Zigadenus densus)*
Cypress spurge *(Euphorbia cyparissias)*
Daffodils *(Narcissus spp.)**
Deadly nightshade *(Atropa belladonna)*
Death camus *(Zigadenus spp.)*
Dumbcane *(Dieffenbachia spp.)**
Dutchman's breeches *(Dicentra spp.)*
Ergot *(Claviceps spp.)*
European bittersweet *(Solanum dulcamara)*
False hellebore *(Veratrum spp.)*
False sago palm *(Cycas revoluta)**
Fly poison *(Amianthemum muscaetoxicum)*
Foxglove *(Digitalis purpurea)*
Groundsel *(Senecio spp.)*
Halogeton *(Halogeton glomeratus)*
Horse chestnut *(Aeseulus spp.)**
Iris *(Iris spp.)*

{ flora }

Hydrangea *(Hydrangea* spp.*)*
Hyacinth *(Hyacinthus orientalus)* *
Jack-in-the-pulpit *(Arisaema* spp.*)*
Jimsonweed *(Datura stramonium)*
Lamb's-quarters *(Chenopodium album)*
Larkspur *(Delphinium* spp.*)*
Lily-of-the-valley *(Convallaria majalis)*
Locoweed *(Astragalus* spp. or *Oxytropis* spp.*)*
Lupine *(Lupinus* spp.*)*
Mayapple *(Podophyllum peltatum)*
Milkweed *(Asclepias* spp.*)*
Mistletoe *(Phoradendron* spp.*)*
Monkshood *(Aconitum* spp.*)*
Mountain laurel *(Kalmia* spp.*)*
Oaks *(Quercus* spp.*)*
Oleander *(Nerium oleander)* *
Onion *(Allium cepa)* *
Philodendron *(Philodendron* spp.*)* *
Pigweed *(Amaranthus species)*
Poison hemlock *(Conium maculatum)*
Poison ivy *(Toxicodendron radicans)*
Poison oak (Eastern) *(Toxicodendron toxicarium)*
Poison sumac *(Toxicodendron vernix)*
Pokeweed *(Phytolacca americana)*
Potato *(Solanum tuberosum)*
Precatory bean *(Abrus precatorius)*
Red maple *(Acer rubrum)*
Rhododendron *(Rhododendron maximum)* *
Rhubarb *(Rheum* spp.*)*
Rosary pea *(Abrus precatorius)*
Sensitive fern *(Onoclea sensibilis)*
Skunk cabbage *(Symplocarpus foetidus)*
Snake plant or mother-in-law's tongue *(Sansevieria* spp.*)* *

Snow-on-the-mountain *(Euphorbia marginata)*
Spurge nettle *(Cnidoscolus stimulosus)*
Star-of-Bethlehem (*Ornithogalum umbellatum*)
Stinging nettle *(Urtica* spp.*)*
Sweet clover *(Melilotus* spp.*)*
Sweet pea *(Lathyrus* spp.*)*
Thorn apple *(Datura stramonium)*
Tomato *(Lycopersicon esculentum)*
Tung-oil tree *(Aleurites* spp.*)* *
Water hemlock *(Cicuta* spp.*)*
White snakeroot *(Eupatorium rugosum)*
Wild bleeding heart *(Dicentra* spp.*)*
Wisteria *(Wisteria* spp.*)*
Wood nettle *(Laportea canadensis)*
Yesterday, today, and tomorrow *(Brunfelsia* spp.*)* *
Yellow jessamine *(Gelsemium* spp.*)*
Yellow oleander (*Thevetia* spp.)*
Yew *(Taxus* spp.*)* *

Sneezes and Wheezes

Allergic reactions to plants' pollen (allergic rhinitis) produce the typical symptoms of sneezing, nasal discharge (runny nose), congestion, and an itchy nose and throat. Seasonal allergic rhinitis occurs during pollen seasons in the spring, summer, and fall. Perennial allergic rhinitis has the same symptoms, but they occur year-round and are triggered by molds, dust, mites, feathers, and animal dander. The common name "hay fever" was coined about 150 years ago because reactions of this type were frequent during the hay-harvesting season, but hay is usually not the allergen that causes the difficulties.

Although goldenrod (*Solidago* spp.) and pine (*Pinus* spp.) are often mistaken for allergy culprits, ragweed (*Ambrosia* spp.) is a much more likely offender. In late summer or early fall ragweed pollen arises to cause misery for many. Ragweed is found throughout the lower 48 states on dry fields, pastures, roadsides, and construction sites, and you can find ragweed on every other continent except Antarctica. Ragweed pollen is just about impossible to avoid because it is so small, entering your home through tiny cracks. If your doors or windows are open

{ flora }

185

to savor the last of summer, you can guess the results. One plant can generate one million grains of pollen, but fewer than 1,000 grains in your bedroom can trigger an allergic reaction. Just about all you can do is resort to over-the counter, prescription, or natural substances to try to alleviate the symptoms.

Christmas Cheer

You may note that poinsettias are not on the danger list above. Widely reported to be highly toxic, the common variety sold widely at Christmas time is not poisonous to people or animals. The confusion stems from the fact that this red flowering beauty is a branch member of the African milk plant family, which does have some extremely lethal specimens. In African folk culture these deadly specimens are sometimes referred to as "husband medicine" for women who want to "cure" themselves of their unwanted attachment.

Mistletoe, however, is another package altogether. All parts of mistletoe are considered potentially toxic, but the berries are especially to be avoided as they have caused death in humans. Children, in particular, might be tempted to sample the small white spheres.

Plants and Child First Aid

The *Poisons and Antidotes Sourcebook* (2nd. Ed.) by Carol Turkington is an excellent resource that every home with children should have. It offers this advice if you think your child has eaten a plant:

- ☞ Stay calm and check your child for adverse reactions.
- ☞ Determine how much of the plant and what part (berries, stem, leaves) your child has eaten.
- ☞ Remove any uneaten plant material from the child's mouth. Check the mouth for redness, blisters, swelling, irritation, and cuts.
- ☞ Observe for allergic reactions: blotchy, red skin; swelling; breathing problems; nausea and diarrhea.
- ☞ Identify the plant. If someone else is in the house, send him or her to a nursery to identify the plant if you don't know its name.
- ☞ Call the poison control center. The phone number for the Chicago Drug and Poison Information Centers are:

Chicago Area Poison Resource Center	**AAPCC Certified Illinois Poison Center**
Medical Center	**222 South Riverside Plaza, Suite 1900**
1753 West Congress Parkway	**Chicago, IL 60606**
Chicago IL 60612	**Emergency Phone: (800) 222-1222;**
(312) 942-5969	**(312) 906-6185 (TTY/TDD)**

- You may also call a national hotline, (800) 222-1222, and you will be connected to a center that serves your area.
- Report any adverse reactions and give age and weight of child.
- If told to go to a hospital, take the plant or a sample with you.
- If your child is too young to speak, retrace the child's steps and check for any damaged plants. If there is plant material in the mouth try to match it with a plant in the area.

Safe Plants

Turkington has thoughtfully compiled the list of safe plants below so that your home and gardens can still be beautiful and trouble free if you are the parents of young children:

African violet	Creeping Charlie	Petunia
Aluminum plant	Dahlia	Poinsettia
Aspidistra	Dandelion	Prayer plant
Aster	Easter lily	Purple passion
Baby's tears	Gardenia	Rose
Begonia	Impatiens	Sensitive plant
Bird's nest fern	Jade plant	Swedish ivy
Boston fern	Lipstick plant	Tiger lily
Bougainvillea	Magnolia	Umbrella tree
California poppy	Marigold	Violet
Camellia	Nasturtium	Wandering Jew
Christmas cactus	Norfolk Island pine	Wild strawberry
Coleus spider plant	Peperomia	Zebra plant

POISON IVY, POISON OAK, AND POISON SUMAC

Billy Ward got it right when he wrote the classic lyrics for "Poison Ivy," the Coasters' 1959 #1 R&B hit. Sometimes it seems like "an ocean of calamine lotion" won't begin to be enough when poison ivy gets under your skin, driving you mad with its relentless itch. Estimates vary, but somewhere between 50 to 85 percent of Americans can relate to Billy Ward's time-honored tune because they are allergic to poison ivy, oak, and sumac—three cousins of the cashew family that in combination are found virtually throughout the lower 48 states. This trio is reported to be the single most common cause of allergic reactions in the U.S. That

{ flora }

means millions (estimates range from 2 to 50 million) of folks each year have a painful, irritating contact dermatitis (varying degrees of itching, swelling, redness, blisters) in reaction to urushiol (pronounced oo-roo-shee-ohl), an oil that is in all parts of the plants: leaves, stems, berries, and especially the sap.

Urushiol is a clear or slightly yellow resin that comes from the Japanese word for "lacquer." While the urushiol is slightly different in the three plants, it is similar enough so that people who have an allergic reaction to one will have an allergic reaction to another. For this reason, what we say about poison ivy here will also apply to the other two species unless otherwise indicated. The profiles at the end of this chapter will help you to identify them individually.

Leaves of Three?

Actually, it isn't leaves you are counting, but leaflets; nonetheless this is a good place to start identifying the poison cashew crew. The famous saying "leaves of three, let it be" is a good rule to follow, but some plants don't always play by the rules. Poison sumac, for example, has 7–13 leaflets. To help you avoid these itch-producing plants, here's a quick overview of their characteristics:

Poison Ivy

☛ Grows around lakes and streams in the Chicago area, but also favors mixed forest grounds and forest edges.

☛ Can be a woody, hairy, rope-like vine, a trailing shrub on the ground, or a freestanding shrub.

☛ Normally has three leaflets (groups of leaves all on the same small stem coming off the larger main stem), but may vary from groups of three to nine.

BED OF POISON IVY

188

- Has leaves that are green in the summer and red in the fall.
- Has yellow or green flowers and white berries.

Poison Oak
- Is found in the Chicago area as a low shrub, generally in well-drained, upland sites.
- Has hair on its fruit, stem, and leaves.
- Has oak-like leaves, each with three leaflets.
- Has clusters of yellowish berries.

Poison Sumac
- Is found in the Chicago area growing in boggy areas, also in bay swamps and the margins of ponds.
- Is a rangy shrub up to 15 feet tall.
- Has 7 to 13 smooth-edged leaflets.
- Has glossy pale yellow or cream-colored berries.

How Do You Get Poison Ivy?

You can get contact dermatitis from poison ivy only by coming in contact with the urushiol (sap) that is released when the plant is bruised or crushed. Although that sounds easy enough to avoid, the plant is delicate and easily bruised on contact—with anything. "Poison oak, ivy, and sumac are very fragile plants," says William L. Epstein, M.D., professor of dermatology, University of California, San Francisco. "Stems or leaves broken by the wind or animals, and even the tiny holes made by chewing insects, can release urushiol."

Here's a typical scenario of how you might "mysteriously" get poison ivy: You use a garden tool to work around an area that has poison ivy, and the tool touches the plant. You clean the tool with a cloth (you always clean all your tools after using them, don't you?), and then wipe your hands and arms with that cloth. Chances are you will get poison ivy. Why? The urushiol contaminates anything it touches: clothing, tools, sports and camping equipment such as sleeping bags, and even some of your dearest friends as you will understand from the following story:

Edith didn't know if she was allergic to poison ivy when she started clearing the overgrown yard of her first home purchase. Fairly aware of the "leaflets of three" guiding principle, she was careful about touching the plants directly and always wore gloves and long sleeves when working in the yard. She had already tried to target the worst patches of poison ivy with Roundup, which kills plants by absorption through the leaves, but some remained. In the early fall she started to rake the yard.

{ flora }

It was still hot and when she started to perspire, she wiped the side of her face and brow with her sleeve. What she didn't know was that poison ivy leaves were in the bundles she was lifting and that they had touched her shirtsleeves. She awoke the next morning to a red, swollen, puffy, itching face that had developed dermatitis in reaction to the urushiol. The fact that the oil was on the tender skin of her face made the situation worse. Urushiol had been transferred from her shirt to her face as she repeatedly wiped the sweat away with her shoulder and forearm. Her allergic reaction was so severe she could barely see out of one eye, so she had to resort to a round of steroids prescribed by a doctor to diminish her body's strong reaction. Edith vowed to be more careful of contact in the future, and she was. She was innocently (and quite mistakenly) relieved when winter took its toll on the remaining plants, thinking that at last, like the ticks, they were out of her life until spring. She was lucky the rest of that year and was extremely careful to avoid plant contact when doing yard work that next spring, summer, and fall until . . .

The next winter when freezing temperatures had been the norm for weeks, she awoke one morning to a disturbingly familiar itching, swelling, and general aggravation on the inside of her lower arms. She wondered, "Poison ivy? In February when I haven't done any yard work for months?" Yes, it was poison ivy. She had gotten it by loving some of her furry best friends. Although she had eradicated almost all of the plants in her fenced-in yard, her cats still went into the neighboring woods where the understory was a virtual carpet of poison ivy quite recognizable in the spring and summer. The cats picked up the oil on their fur, and when she picked up the cats to carry them with bare arms, she contacted the urushiol just as if she had had direct contact with the plant itself, so another systemic round of poison ivy ensued. The good news is that Edith didn't have outbreaks on her hands because the skin of the palms (and soles) is thicker, so the oil does not usually penetrate these areas.

In another example, Joan also contracted a serious bout of poison ivy when her clothes touched the clothes of her husband, Bob, after he had been mountain biking. Although Bob had no sensitivity to the plant, his clothes carried the oil home to Joan, who had left the house that weekend only to go shopping for quilt fabric at the mall.

Points of Contact

To reiterate, contact with urushiol can occur in three ways:
- ☞ Direct contact—touching the sap of the toxic plant.
- ☞ Indirect contact—touching something to which urushiol has spread. The oil can stick to the fur of animals, to garden tools or

sports equipment, or to any objects that have come into contact with a crushed or broken plant.

☛ In another form of indirect contact, airborne urushiol particles, such as from burning plants, may come in contact with your skin or respiratory system.

When Can You Get Poison Ivy?

As we see from Edith's story, you can get poison ivy at any time of year. The urushiol is more potent in the spring and summer when the plants are most vibrant, but the dead of winter will do just fine, too. The oil also has real staying power, remaining active for up to a year or more on the surface that was touched. So a hunter who had the oil on his camouflage jacket last year can get poison ivy again this year before he even steps out of the house—just by putting on his jacket.

Paddlers and Others, Step Lively

Poison ivy—and its cousin poison oak—have an insidious way of wreaking havoc on the simplest adventure, be it a hike in the woods or a picnic in a park. Even when water is the dominant environment, poison ivy may lurk along riverbanks, so paddlers need to be alert, too. The damage is usually done while traipsing to put-ins and away from take-outs, while scouting or portaging when your concentration is more focused on rocks and rivers than rash-causing flora. Countless waterways hide the vicious vine along their shores. Watch your step—and add calamine or some other soothing option (see page 195) to your equipment list.

AUTUMN POISON OAK

{ flora }

191

Relative Sensitivity

The poison ivy rash can affect almost any part of your body, especially in places where your skin is thin, such as on your face or on the inside of your arms, but is less likely to manifest on the thicker-skinned areas (such as palms and soles).

Sensitivity may occur after only one exposure, but usually people develop sensitivity to poison ivy, oak, or sumac only after several encounters with the plants, sometimes over many years. About 85 percent of all people will develop an allergic reaction when adequately exposed to poison ivy.

Sensitivity varies from person to person. People who reach adulthood without becoming sensitive have only a 50 percent chance of developing an allergy to poison ivy. Sensitivity to poison ivy tends to decline with age. Children who have reacted to poison ivy will probably find that their sensitivity decreases by half by young adulthood without repeated exposure. People who were once allergic to poison ivy may even lose their sensitivity later in life. Some people are very sensitive to poison ivy, developing a severe rash with blisters and extreme swelling on their face, arms, legs, and genitals. Such severe cases need medical treatment sooner rather than later.

When assessing whether or not to get medical treatment consider:

If you have had strong reactions in the past you are likely, but not guaranteed, to have strong reactions in the future.

The characteristics of the rash outbreak including location (as above), degree of severity, and amount of body affected. Even if the rash does not appear to be severe, the greater the area affected, then the greater the need for medical care.

Avoiding Exposure to Poison Ivy

The American Academy of Dermatology recommends that whenever you're going to be around poison ivy—trying to clear it from your yard or hiking in the woods—wear long pants and long sleeves and, if possible, gloves and boots. And must we add, don't wipe with vegetation? Drip dry.

If You Have Been Exposed to Poison Ivy

Because urushiol can penetrate the skin within minutes, there's no time to waste if you know you've been exposed. "The earlier you cleanse the skin, the greater the chance that you can remove the urushiol before it gets attached to the skin," says Hon-Sum Ko, M.D., an allergist and immunologist with the Food and Drug Administration's Center for Drug Evaluation and Research. Cleansing may not stop the initial outbreak of the rash if more than 10 minutes has elapsed, but it can help prevent further spread.

If you've been exposed to poison ivy, oak, or sumac, if possible, stay outdoors until you complete the first two following steps:

☞ First, cleanse exposed skin with generous amounts of isopropyl (rubbing) alcohol. Don't return to the woods or yard the same day. Alcohol removes your skin's protection along with the urushiol and any new contact will cause the urushiol to penetrate twice as fast. The resin is soluble in alcohol, and some say that beer or other alcoholic beverages will help remove the resin from the skin. If you have none of these substances, go to the next step.

☞ Wash skin with cold water. Do not scrub with a brush. Remove rings, bracelets, and such before washing hands. Wash jewelry. First rely more on rinsing and less on soaping because immediately after contact the soap might increase distribution of the fresh urushiol.

☞ A solution of baking soda and water may also be helpful. If the oil has been on the skin for less than six hours, thorough cleansing with cold water and strong soap, repeated three times, will usually prevent reaction.

☞ Third, take a regular shower with soap and warm water. Do not take a bath, because that will only distribute the oil all over your body.

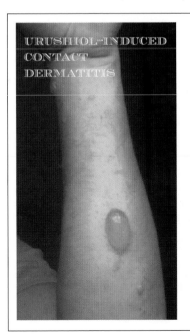
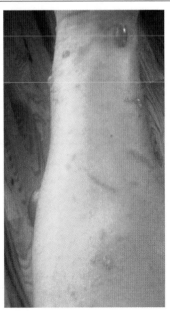

URUSHIOL-INDUCED CONTACT DERMATITIS

{ flora }

- Clothes, shoes, tools, and anything else that may have been in contact with the urushiol should be wiped off with alcohol and water. The palms of the hands rarely break out in a rash because of the thickness of the skin, but hands can still be contaminated with the plant's oil. The problem with getting the oil on your hands is that you carry it to other surfaces. Touch yourself anywhere and the rash spreads. You rub your cheek, scratch your ear or your back, go to the bathroom, or pull off your socks—and you've spread the oil to all those spots. Wear gloves when handling contaminated clothing or tools and then discard the hand covering.

- The oil can also travel around on your clothes. Contaminated clothing should be washed separately. Once you've showered and washed all contaminated areas and articles, the rash can no longer spread to other parts of your body or to anyone else. Make sure you wash all clothes and shoes with hot water and a strong soap. If you bring the clothes into your house, be careful that you do not transfer the urushiol to rugs or furniture. You may also dry-clean contaminated clothes. Bathe pets that have come in contact with poison ivy, oak, or sumac because the sap can stay on them for days.

- Because urushiol can remain active for months, wash camping, sporting, fishing, or hunting gear that was in contact with the oil.

Tec Lab Solutions

God and the doctors know (notice they are different), I've had some strong reactions to poison ivy. While there are many good products on the market to help folks through the event, personal experience has led me to Tec Labs products. They have a line of protection and cleansing products. Calagel is their answer to calamine lotion. Aside from being an effective itch stopper, it doesn't make you look like a pink, flaking alien with a weird case of psoriasis. The company's website (teclabsinc. com) explains that Tec Lab "has been protecting consumers and industrial workers since 1977. . . . The flagship Tec Labs product, Tecnu®, was developed in 1961 during the Cold War era by chemical engineer Dr. Robert Smith as a waterless cleanser for removing radioactive dust from the skin and clothing. His wife accidentally discovered that Tecnu would remove poison plant oils after exposure to poison oak and ivy." (Talk about industrial strength!)

The Tec Labs website has good information on the poison ivy product line, as well as on the company's other repellents and solutions. You can also find out online where you can buy Tec Lab products, but they are fairly widely available

No product, including Tecnu, will make the experience just disappear, but the company's soap and gel can really help.

Symptoms of Poison Ivy Contact Dermatitis

If you don't cleanse quickly enough or if your skin is so sensitive that cleansing didn't help:

- ☞ Redness, rash, and swelling will appear in about 12 to 48 hours. A characteristic pattern is a line of reaction, as if you had made a streaking mark with a pen or pencil tipped with the allergen oil.
- ☞ Blisters and itching will follow.
- ☞ Blisters will peak about five days after exposure and then break and ooze clear fluid, crust over, and eventually heal in another week or two, even without treatment.

For those rare people who react after their very first exposure, the rash appears after 7 to 10 days.

Treating the Rash and Itch

Because they don't contain urushiol, the oozing blisters are not contagious nor can the fluid cause further spread on the affected person's body. Nevertheless, don't scratch the blisters because your fingernails may carry germs that could cause an infection in the open sores.

The rash doesn't spread across the body and will only occur where urushiol has touched the skin. However, the rash may seem to spread if it appears over time instead of all at once. This is either because the urushiol is absorbed at different rates in different parts of the body or because of repeated exposure to contaminated objects, such as urushiol trapped under the fingernails.

The rash, blisters, and itch normally disappear in 14 to 20 days without any treatment, but most people need some itch relief.

For mild cases, wet compresses or soaking in cool water may be effective.

- ☞ Oral antihistamines, such as over-the-counter remedies like Benadryl, can also relieve itching.
- ☞ Over-the-counter topical hydrocortisone compounds (such as Cortaid and Lanacort) with 1 percent or less of hydrocortisone are generally not considered to be effective.
- ☞ For severe cases, prescription topical corticosteroid drugs can halt the reaction, but only if treatment begins within a few hours of exposure.
- ☞ A tepid bath with oatmeal or colloidal Aveeno can help. If your skin's too sore for you to go to the store, run some uncooked rolled

{ flora }

195

oats through the blender till you have a fine flour. Sprinkle that in the bath and get in it—reportedly it substantially reduces the itching.

☞ For those who prefer more natural alternatives, jewelweed (untested by the author) applied by rubbing the plant on affected areas is commonly listed as an in-the-field treatment to break down the urushiol. It almost goes without saying that you need to be absolutely sure you know your jewelweed before you use it. You can also purchase a line of jewelweed products, such as soap from Alternative Nature Online Herbal at altnature.com (Karen Bergeron, AltNature Herbals, P.O. Box 93, Erin, TN 37061). For orders call (877) 753-0087. Otherwise, please email karen@altnature.com. I haven't tried this soap, but it sounds worth investigating.

☞ Rhuli anti-itch gel made with camphor is another general transparent itch treatment for bites, stings, and the like that is favored by those who prefer "alternative medicine." Rhuli is good, but Tecnu's Clearly Calagel is tougher. Both are found at drugstores.

☞ Naturopathic remedies include jewelweed juice, which is contained in Oak-Away. This product also contains mugwort, goldenseal, comfrey, and chickweed. Both Oak-Away and the homeopathic formula Hyland's PoisonIvy/Oak are available at health food stores. A homeopathic remedy worth trying as a preventative contains Rhus toxicodendron 6X (poison ivy/poison oak), Croton tiglium 6X (croton oil), and Xerophyllum 6X (basket grass flower).

☞ A short-term but effective fix is a really hot bath or shower. Heat releases histamine, the substance in the skin that causes itching. Extremely hot water will cause intense itching as the histamine is released, but the itching subsides as the skin becomes depleted of histamine. However, as cited above, do not use a bath to initially rid your body of the urushiol oil.

☞ If you have had severe reactions in the past and know you have been exposed, it's a good idea to contact medical help, such as your dermatologist, as soon as possible after a new exposure. He or she can help to lessen the effects of your body's allergic reaction before it gets "carried away."

☞ Severe reactions can be treated with prescription oral corticosteroids, such as prednisone. Oral corticosteroids may be especially appropriate if the rash is on the face, genitals, or covers more than 30 percent of the body. The drug must be taken for several days, commonly 10 to 14 days. Topical steroid creams are less effective than oral systemic treatment, but the oral varieties can make you feel like Arnold Schwarzenegger, all armored up and no place to annihilate.

The FDA recommends a number of OTC (over-the-counter) products to help dry up the oozing blisters:

- aluminum acetate (Burows solution)

baking soda	Aveeno (oatmeal bath)
aluminum hydroxide gel	calamine
kaolin	zinc acetate
zinc carbonate	zinc oxide

Preventive Medicine

The FDA has recently approved some barrier creams (bentoquatam—a topical skin protectant used to prevent or reduce allergic contact dermatitis from contact with poison ivy, oak, and sumac). Our friends at Tec Labs have created a barrier solution to be applied *before* exposure, when you know you're going into poison ivy country. I don't know how effective it is, but based on the company's reputation, it's worth a try. If it is effective, it's a real breakthrough because preventative measures have been sought for decades. Two other barrier products (not tested by the author) are IvyBlock and Work Shield.

Prescription pills can provide immunization, but this treatment takes months to achieve reasonable hyposensitization. It also has a track record of some substantial side effects such as skin problems, stomach problems, fever, inflammation, and convulsions. For these reasons, only folks, such as firefighters, who have a lot of contact with poison ivy as a course of duty, are the best candidates. Contact your dermatologist for more information.

Good Riddance

There are really only two solutions for ridding your surroundings of poison ivy: chemical and manual.

Herbicides can chemically do the job, but the FDA advises that the two herbicides most commonly used for poison ivy—Roundup and Ortho Poison Ivy Killer—will kill other plants as well. Spraying Roundup (active ingredient glyphosate) on the foliage of young plants will kill the poison ivy, but if the poison ivy vine is growing up your prize rhododendron or azalea, for example, the Roundup will kill them too.

{ flora }

Joseph Neal, Ph.D., associate professor of weed science at Cornell University, advises, "Ortho Poison Ivy Killer (active ingredient triclopyr), if used sparingly, will kill poison ivy, but not the trees it grows around. Don't use it around shrubs, broad-leaf ground cover, or herbaceous garden plants. It is possible to spray the poison ivy without killing other plants if you pull the poison ivy vines away from the desirable plants and wipe the ivy foliage with the herbicide, or use a shield on the sprayer to direct the chemical."

If you don't want to use chemicals, manual removal will get rid of the ivy, but you must be diligent and get every bit of the plant—leaves, vines, and roots—or it will sprout again. Obviously, manual removal has its own hazards. Wear plastic gloves over cotton gloves when pulling the plants. Plastic alone isn't enough because the plastic rips, and cotton alone won't work because after a while the urushiol will soak through.

Check local regulations to see how the plants can be safely and legally disposed. Urushiol will break down with composting, but the plants must be chopped into small pieces first, which just adds to your risk of exposure.

Never burn poison ivy. The smoke is also toxic and can irritate the noses, throats, lungs, eyes, and faces of those who come in contact with it.

Shape Shifters for All Seasons

Poison ivy can have different forms. It grows as a crawling vine, a climbing vine, or low shrub. Poison oak, with its leaflets resembling oak leaves, is a low shrub in the Chicago area, but can be a low or high shrub in the western U.S. Poison sumac grows to a tall shrub or small tree.

Because they are year-round hazards, know how to recognize these toxic plants in all seasons. In the early fall, the leaves can turn colors such as yellow or red when other plants are still green. The berry-like fruit on the mature female plants also changes color in fall, from green to off-white, and in the winter the plants lose their leaves. In the spring, poison ivy has yellow-green flowers.

CONTACT URTICARIA

No, this isn't a commando's directive in a B-grade science fiction film. "Urticaria" is from the Latin word for nettle, a plant with toothed leaves covered with hairs that have a stinging fluid. The other Latin root at work here is "uro," the word for "burn," in the sense of a chafing, irritating, rubbing sore. Contact urticaria occurs when you touch plants such as nettles whose broken hairs then inject a stinging toxin into your skin. The most common causes of contact urticaria in the U.S. are from rubbing against or handling stinging nettles, spurge nettles, bull nettles, or wood nettles. Although the sensation is unpleasant, the effects are usually not serious nor long lasting. Prevention is best achieved through awareness of the nettle-type plants and subsequent avoidance. If necessary, antihistamines such as Benadryl may be useful, but in situations of extreme anaphylactic reactions, epinephrine administration (as from a bee sting kit) is required.

Poison Ivy (Toxicodendron radicans)

- Exposure to poison ivy causes mild to severe (including systemic) contact dermatitis for allergic individuals.
- It is common throughout the eastern U.S.
- It may take the forms of a ground cover, trailing vine, climbing vine with hairy rope-like stem, or rarely as a low shrub. Leaves are alternate (not directly opposite each other on the stem) with three leaflets. The plant has green flowers in June and July. Fruits are white and smooth or hairy from August to November. Leaves are green in summer, red in fall. Poison ivy loses its leaves in winter.
- Size varies depending on the form of the plant.
- Poison ivy grows in fertile, well-drained soil in the woods and at their margins; along structures suitable for climbing, such as stone walls; and at the water's edge on rock-strewn shores of rivers and lakes, or on the flood plains of streams.
- Poison ivy is often confused with seedlings of box elder (*Acer negurdo*). Box elder is a maple, and maples have opposite leaves, whereas poison ivy has alternate leaves. Other common plants are often mistaken for poison ivy: hog peanut and Virginia creeper. Hog peanut has three leaflets, but the stem is not woody. Flowers are white to lilac-colored. Virginia creeper has five leaflets and produces blush-colored berries.

POISON IVY

Eastern Poison Oak (Toxicodendron toxicarium)

- Eastern poison oak causes mild to severe (including systemic) contact dermatitis for allergic individuals.
- It is common in the eastern U.S.
- Poison oak is an upright bushy shrub that sometimes takes a vine-like appearance. Branches are rigid and smooth. Leaves are alternate and compound with three leaflets that are oval-shaped or evenly lobed, shiny, and reminiscent of oak leaves. Fruit is white and smooth.
- It grows to 3 to 6 feet in height as an upright shrub.
- It grows in sandy soils in acid woods, sometimes near lakes.
- Unlike poison ivy, poison oak is never a climbing vine. It is also, like poison ivy, confused with hog peanut and Virginia creeper stem.

POISON OAK

{ flora }

201

Poison Sumac (Toxicodendron vernix)

- Exposure causes mild to severe (including systemic) contact dermatitis for allergic individuals.
- Common in the eastern U.S.
- Poison sumac grows as a small tree or shrub with alternate pinnately (feather-patterned) compound leaves of 7 to 13 smooth-edged leaflets. Smooth, white fruit from August to November.
- It grows to 6 to 20 feet.
- Poison sumac tends to grow in wet soil near standing water, such as peat bogs, swampy pinewoods, bay swamps, edges of ponds, or acidic creek bottoms.

POISON SUMAC

Stinging Nettle (*Urtica dioica L.*)

- This plant stings on contact.
- It is found throughout much of the U.S, and is commonly found in the eastern U.S.
- This perennial has four angled stems. Lower stems have stinging hairs. Leaves are roughly heart-shaped. Greenish flowers bloom from June to September.
- It grows to 1 to 4 feet in height.
- It grows in moist thickets and waste areas.
- The lower stems especially have stinging hairs that break off on contact and inject a burning chemical mixture into the skin. The sensation may last for up to an hour.

STINGING NETTLE

{ flora }

Cow Parsnip (Heracleum maximum)

- This plant stings on contact.
- It is a tall herb, reaching to heights of over 6 feet. The genus name *Heracleum* (from "Hercules") refers to the very large size of all parts of these plants. Cow parsnip has the characteristic flowers of the carrot family. These may be flat-topped or more rounded and are always white. Sometimes the outer flowers of the umbel are much larger than the inner ones. The leaves are very large, up to 8 inches across, divided into lobes. The stems are stout and succulent.
- The juices of all parts contain a phototoxin that can act on contact with skin and exposure to ultraviolet light, causing anything from a mild rash to a blistering, severe dermatitis, depending on the sensitivity of the individual. The plant is a pernicious weed, especially in pastures, where it can ruin the milk of cows that eat it.
- Various Native American peoples had many different uses for this plant. All parts of it were used by one nation or another.

COW PARSNIP

Bibliography

Mammals

Adler, Bill Jr. 1992. *Outwitting Critters: A Surefire Manual for Confronting Devious Animals and Winning.* New York: The Lyons Press.

The California Center for Wildlife with Diana Landau and Shelley Stump. 1994. *Living with Wildlife: How to Enjoy, Cope with, and Protect North America's Wild Creatures Around Your Home and Theirs.* San Francisco. Sierra Club Books.

Insects and Arachnids

Arnett, Ross H., Jr. 2000. *American Insects: A Handbook of the Insects of America North of Mexico. 2ed.* Boca Raton, Florida: CRC Press.

Auerbach, Paul S. 2011. *Wilderness Medicine.* Philadelphia: Elsevier.

Berenbaum, May R. 1995. *Bugs in the System: Insects and Their Impact on Human Affairs.* Reading, Massachusetts. Perseus Books.

Hillyard, Paul. 1994. *The Book of the Spider: From Arachnophobia to the Love of Spiders.* New York: Random House.

Hubbell, Sue. 1993. *Broadsides from the Other Orders: A Book of Bugs.* New York: Random House.

Reptiles and Amphibians

Carr, Archie Fairly. *Handbook of Turtles: The Turtles of the United States, Canada, and Baja California.* 1995: Cornell University Press.

Klauber, Lawrence Monroe, and Harry W. Greene. 1997. *Rattlesnakes: Their Habits, Life Histories, and Influence on Mankind.* Berkeley: University of California Press.

Rubio, Mann. 1998. *Rattlesnake: Portrait of a Predator.* D.C.: Smithsonian Institution Press.

Plants

Caras, Roger and Steven Foster. *1994. A Field Guide to Venomous Animals and Poisonous Plants: North America North of Mexico.* New York: Houghton Mifflin Company (Peterson Field Guides).

Turkington, Carol A. 1998. *The Poisons and Antidotes Sourcebook.* New York: Facts on File, Inc.

Photo Credits

p. viii—clockwise (starting with snake)—Rich Phallin/iStockphoto .com; (poison ivy) Oliver Childs/iStockphoto.com; (owl) Jill Lang/iStock photo.com; (deer) Paul Tessler/iStockphoto.com; (hawk) Mark Wilson/ iStockphoto.com; (bee) Elena Asenova/iStockphoto.com.

Mammals

p. 18—U.S. Fish & Wildlife Service National Digital Library; p. 20—Wiki commons/Darkone; p. 22—Wikicommons; p. 27—U.S. Fish & Wildlife Service National Digital Library/Steve Thompson; p. 35—U.S. Fish & Wildlife Service National Digital Library/Don Pfitzer; p. 42—U.S. Fish & Wildlife Service National Digital Library/Greg Thompson; p. 48—U.S. Fish & Wildlife Service National Digital Library; pp. 50–51, Wikicommons.

Insects

p. 54—©Carl Wiens; p. 58—©Carl Wiens; p. 57—Hansoner/ iStockphoto .com; p. 64—Joseph Berger, Bugwood.org; p. 66—David Cappaert, Michigan State University, Bugwood.org; p. 70—Russ Ottens, University of Georgia, Bugwood.org; p. 72—David Cappaert, Michigan State University, Bugwood.org; p. 73 (black-and-yellow mud dauber)—Wikicommons/Higu, (bumblebee)—Willi Schmitz/iStockphoto.com; p. 74—Wikicommons; p. 75—Wikicommons; p. 77—Clemson University–USDA Cooperative Extension Slide Series, Bugwood.org; p. 78—Clemson University–USDA Cooperative Extension Slide Series, Bugwood.org; p. 81—Wikicommons/ Gilles San Martin; p. 85—Centers for Disease Control and Prevention Public Health Control Library; p. 90—Dr. Ken Walker, Pest and Diseases Image Library, Bugwood.org; p. 93—Wikicommons; p. 96—Wikicommons; p. 99—Wikicommons/Dennis Ray; p. 100—Wikicommons; p. 101—Wikicommons; p. 102—Wikicommons; p. 104, Wikicommons; p. 105—Wikicommons; p. 106—(top) Whitney Cranshaw, Bugwood .org, (bottom) Bastiaan M. Drees/Texas; p. 107—A&M University; Joseph Burger, Bugwood.org; p. 109—Joseph Burger, Bugwood.org; p. 110— Eugene E. Nelson, Bugwood.org; p. 113—Joseph Berger, Bugwood.org; p. 119—Wikicommons; p. 122—Scott Bauer, USDA Agricultural Research Service, Bugwood.org; p. 123—Jim Occi, Bug Pics, Bugwood.org; p. 125—Wikicommons; p. 128—Mat Pound, USDA Agricultural Research Service, Bugwood.org; p. 129—Susan Ellis, USDA APHIS PPQ, Bugwood. org; p. 131—Wikicommons; p. 132—Susan Ellis, Bugwood.org; p. 135— Wikicommons; p. 136—Wikicommons; p. 138—Wikicommons; p. 140— Johnny N. Dell, Bugwood.org; p. 141 (top)—David Cappaert, Michigan State University, Bugwood.org, (bottom)—Gerald J. Lenhard, Louisana State University, Bugwood.org.

Reptiles

pp. 146–147—Ohio Department of Natural Resources; p. 151—Edward Minigault, Clemson University Donated Collection, Bugwood.org; p. 159—Wikicommons; p. 163—Nathan Reighard/iStockphoto.com; p. 166—Wikicommons.

Birds

p. 172—all photos: Wikicommons; p. 177—Wikicommons; p. 178—(top) Wikicommons; (bottom) Wikicommons; p. 179—(top) Lee Rogers/iStockphoto.com; (bottom) Wikicommons.

Flora

p. 188—M.B. Cheatham/iStockphoto.com; p. 191—Mary Stephens/iStockphoto.com; p. 193—Wikicommons; p. 200—Natural Resources Conservation Service; p. 201—Natural Resources Conservation Service; p. 202—Robert H. Mohlenbrock@ USDA-NRCS PLANTS Database/USDA SCS; p. 203—Wikicommons; p. 204—Wikicommons.

Index

R

S

T

{ index }

213

About the Author

F. LYNNE BACHLEDA has been a freelance researcher and writer for more than 30 years. She has applied her expertise as a generalist to wide-ranging subjects— nature, storytelling, sports, local history, religion, pup- pets, and civil rights, to name a few. She specializes in developing interpretive content for museums, and has been a teaching artist, principally for the Tennessee Performing Arts Center, since 1988. She has authored nine books, and three of these have been accorded national awards. She is also a play- wright. For more information: onemindthinking.net.